P9-DHZ-696

EX LIBRIS
TSM

REDWOOD
LIBRARY

WITHDRAWN

HAMPTON
COURT PALACE

HAMPTON
COURT PALACE

MATTHEW STURGIS

Matthew Sturgis

1X/99.

CHANNEL 4 BOOKS

First published in 1998 by Channel 4 Books, an imprint
of Macmillan Publishers Ltd, 25 Eccleston Place,
London SW1W 9NF and Basingstoke.

Associated companies throughout the world.

ISBN 0 7522 1319 9

Text © Matthew Sturgis, 1998

The right of Matthew Sturgis to be identified as the author of
this work has been asserted by him in accordance with the
Copyright, Designs and Patents Act 1988.

All rights reserved. No part of this publication may be
reproduced, stored in or introduced into a retrieval system,
or transmitted, in any form, or by any means (electronic,
mechanical, photocopying, recording or otherwise) without the
prior written permission of the publisher. Any person who
does any unauthorized act in relation to this publication may
be liable to criminal prosecution and civil claims for damage.

9 8 7 6 5 4 3 2 1

A CIP catalogue record for this book is available from the
British Library.

Design by Isobel Gillan
Colour reproduction by Speedscan Limited
Printed in Italy by New Interlitho
Picture credits can be found on page 192

This book is sold subject to the condition that it shall not, by
way of trade or otherwise, be lent, re-sold, hired out, or
otherwise circulated without the publisher's prior consent in
any form of binding or cover other than that in which it is
published and without a similar condition including this
condition being imposed on the subsequent publisher.

BAZAL

This book accompanies the television series *Hampton Court
Palace* made by Bazal (part of GMG Endemol Entertainment)
for Channel 4.
Executive producer: Nikki Cheetham
Series Editor: Annette Clarke

Sept 08, 1992

CONTENTS

CHAPTER 1

A PLEASANT SITE

*H*ampton Court has long been a favoured place of habitation. Set on the north bank of the River Thames, it stands some thirteen miles west of Westminster, where the narrowness of the stream affords a reliable crossing-place. A manor has existed on the site since Saxon times, when nearby Kingston was the site for the royal coronations. On the eve of the Norman Conquest it was in the possession of Earl Algar. He did not survive the coming of the Conqueror and, under the new dynasty, the manor of 'Hamntone' passed to Walter de St Valeri, one of William's knights. It was clearly a pleasant and prosperous place, with its 2,000 acres of surrounding land and its fisheries. Its value in the Domesday Book was set at the not insignificant sum of £39.

OPPOSITE Hampton Court viewed from the southeast. ABOVE The oldest thing in the palace: the bell hanging above Anne Boleyn's gateway was salvaged from the Hospitallers' chapel.

The manor remained in the hands of the St Valeri family for over a century and a half. From them it passed to the Knights Hospitallers of St John of Jerusalem, one of the military orders founded during the twelfth century. The Knights built up a network of hospitals across Europe for the care of pilgrims bound for the Holy Land. But, like the Templars, they also grew into a wealthy and independent organization. They took on the manor of Hampton Court not as a hospital or preceptory, but as a working farm. There seems to have been little more than an estate hall, or 'camera', on the moated site before the late-fifteenth century.

The Knights Hospitallers continued as lords of the manor for over 250 years. They farmed the acres and ensured that Hampton Court remained a haven of quiet during the troubled years of Yorkist–Lancastrian strife. The life of the manor seems to have grown, and amongst the barns and outbuildings a chapel was established for the use of the community. With the ending of the Wars of the Roses, Hampton Court began to draw royal notice. Henry VII, after he ascended to the throne following his defeat of Richard III at the Battle of Bosworth, built a country palace for himself at Richmond, just four miles down river from Hampton Court. The manor of Hampton Court made a convenient 'cell', or subsidiary house, near to the palace. He sometimes visited the Knights of St John to use their chapel and enjoy their gardens.

His Queen, the beautiful fair-complexioned Elizabeth of York, perhaps accompanied him on these visits. Certainly in January 1503 she spent a week at Hampton Court, praying in the chapel for the safe delivery of her seventh child. Her prayers were only partially answered: a healthy daughter, Katherine, was born a few weeks later in the royal apartments at the Tower of London, but the Queen herself did not long survive the event; she died just nine days afterwards, aged thirty-seven.

The royal connection with Hampton Court was not broken at her death. Indeed, a few years later a new and stronger tie was forged when Henry's Chamberlain, Sir Giles Daubeney, leased the manor from the Knights for £50 a year, in order to have a base close to the King at Richmond.

Very little is known of the buildings that made up the manor house at this time. There was a dovecote in the garden and a collection of barns, probably arranged around a courtyard, but whether any traces of Saxon, Norman or Gothic architecture survived, it is impossible to know. Daubeney began his own programme of improvements. It was probably he who built the first Hall upon the site. And some traces of other foundation works, possibly dating from his tenure, were found during excavations in the Clock Court during the 1970s; their outline has been marked out in the pavement. But his actual buildings have

all been obliterated by the ambitious building projects of subsequent years.

An inventory drawn up in 1514, when Wolsey took over the lease of Hampton Court, does list amongst the chapel furnishings 'ii bells in the towre'. The tower and the chapel have long since vanished but one of the bells does, it seems, survive. It was rescued and put to work by the new tenants. It now hangs in the little bell-tower above Anne Boleyn's gateway, and tolls the hours given by the great clock. The bell bears two inscriptions: the initials 'T.H.', indicating that it was made by the great fifteenth-century bell-founder, Thomas Harrys; and the Latin imprecation, '+Stella+Maria+Maris+Succurre+Piisimar+Nobis+' ('Mary most holy, Star of the Sea, come to our assistance'), confirming that the Hospitallers' chapel was dedicated to the Blessed Virgin. The sound of this bell, now only rung for funerals, runs as an extraordinary and enduring thread through the long and varied history of Hampton Court.

A Butcher's Son

The founding father of what we now know as Hampton Court Palace was Cardinal Wolsey. It was he who expanded the charming Thames-side manor house into something altogether more splendid. And some of the outline – together with much of the flavour – of what he created is still discernible today.

Thomas Wolsey was one of the great figures of the Tudor age. He had achieved prominence under Henry VII but his advancement became more rapid with the accession of Henry VIII. The young King was devoted to pleasure – to hunting, jousting, tennis, music, poetry and philandering.

He was content to place government business in the hands of his capable councillors, and none was more capable than Wolsey.

Wolsey was the son of an Ipswich butcher. He had risen on merit, following the well-worn career path from Oxford University into the Church. He had won preferment, becoming first a chaplain to the Archbishop of Canterbury and then to the royal household. His energy was prodigious, and so was his genius for administration. At Henry VIII's accession in 1509 Wolsey was about thirty-six. He became a royal councillor. Within a few years he had risen to a position of unrivalled prominence amongst the young King's advisers. He was able to transact business almost without reference to other ministers. His power needed a setting and he soon conceived a series of grandiose building projects as solid manifestations and reflections of his status: a palace in London at York Place, a college at Oxford, and a place of retreat. While considering a suitable location for this last project, his attention was drawn to the manor of Hampton Court.

It was close to London and, no less importantly, it offered the benefits of clear air, clean water and dry, gravelly soil. Wolsey was much concerned with such matters. Already corpulent, his health was under constant attack. He suffered from 'the stone' and from dropsy, a disease in which water collects in the body tissue causing uncomfortable swelling. He was prone too to a host of rather unspecific Tudor ailments such as colic, ague and quinsy. It is said that Wolsey, when beginning his search for a suitable house, had consulted the eminent physicians of the University of Padua and asked them to suggest the most salubrious spot within twenty miles of Westminster; they had recommended Hampton Court.

Cardinal Wolsey.

Wolsey was clearly convinced by their report. On 24 June 1514 he took out a lease on the manor of Hampton Court from the Knights Hospitallers at £50 a year. The lease ran for ninety-nine years with a provision for a further ninety-nine after that. It was a long view for a supposedly celibate clergyman to take – but Wolsey, like many other worldly prelates of the period, took a relaxed attitude to the constraints of clerical celibacy. He had an established mistress and several children.

Nevertheless, Wolsey's motives in taking Hampton Court were less personal than public. If the manor was to be a resort of pleasure, that pleasure was to be ostentatious and impressive. Wolsey's lease – a copy of which can still be seen at the British Library – conferred few obligations upon him. He was required to have Masses said in

the chapel, to keep up the rabbit-warren in the park and maintain the weir, but little else. He was entitled 'to take down, alter, transpose, change, make new byeld at theire propre costs any houses, walles, mootes, diches, warkis, or other things with or about the said manor', as he chose. Wolsey had big plans for his new home – and they got bigger.

England, since the coming of the Tudors, had achieved a new prominence on the European stage. After the internecine strife of the previous decades, peace and sound government had brought wealth and had allowed for the exercise of foreign ambitions. Henry VIII had built upon the achievements of his father. He had won a victory over the French at the 'Battle of the Spurs' and the Scots were defeated at Flodden. He – together with Wolsey – had cut a fine figure at the Field of the Cloth of Gold. Nevertheless, even amidst the glory of that occasion he had become aware of the new sophistication of continental European culture. The artistic ideas of the Renaissance were finding a ready expression in France, most conspicuously perhaps in the great building schemes of Francis I, at Fontainebleau and Chambord. Henry wanted to rival them. Wolsey took up the challenge on his behalf at Hampton Court.

The mighty prelate identified himself so closely with his monarch and his realm that he came to believe that anything that displayed his own importance reflected theirs too. Certainly his wealth was princely, if not regal. Already the Bishop of Lincoln, Durham, Bath, Worcester and Hereford, the Abbot of St Albans and the Grand Almoner of the Royal Household, within a year of acquiring Hampton Court he was appointed Archbishop of York, Lord Chancellor and

The gatehouse: Wolsey's wooden bridge over the moat was replaced with a stone one by Henry VIII.

Cardinal. While not every title conferred duties, they all provided incomes. It was an unprecedented concentration of wealth and power in the hands of a single man. And Hampton Court, Wolsey determined, should be the showcase for this glory.

He demolished most, if not all, of the existing buildings on the site and drew up plans for a magnificent new palace. It was conceived on a grand scale and in a new style.

In that age before architects it was probably Wolsey himself who determined the design of the building. He was assisted no doubt in drawing up his plans by such men as his 'surveyor of buildings', Lawrence Stubbs, by his 'master of the works' and by his 'clerk controller'. The individual master-craftsmen — the master-mason, the master-carpenter and others — would then have had to exercise their imagination and skill in interpreting Wolsey's ideas and making them real.

In conception Wolsey's building was something new. Although he dug a moat around the site (said to be the last moat dug in England), the general flavour of the building was not that of a fortress castle but of a palace. Rather than using stone he built in brick. His bricks were a deep-red, almost purple, colour; and they were quite large: 10 inches x 2 inches x 4½ inches. Every detail existed for show and comfort, not defence.

All modern conveniences were provided. Fresh water was brought from the springs at Hampton village and in the Upper Park. Pipes were laid, and brick conduit houses built, to control and ensure the supply.

Wolsey enclosed 2,000 acres of parkland around the manor with a high well-buttressed brick wall.

The Base Court: once a lodging place for Wolsey's retainers and guests.

The land was divided by the Kingston to Hampton highway into two sections — the Home, or House, Park and Bushy Park. Both the division and the wall survive to this day, and it is possible to see where Wolsey instructed his bricklayers to break up the dark red brickwork with the symbolic motif of the Calvary Cross picked out with black bricks.

Building work progressed rapidly. In less than two years the outline of a palace had sprung up on the banks of the Thames; decoration and furnishing were already under way. By 1517 Hampton Court was ready to receive its first guests — King Henry VIII and his Queen, Catherine of Aragon. They must have been impressed by what they saw.

It was said that — when completed — there were over a thousand rooms in the palace. Wolsey needed them. His own household was substantial and his palace was designed to accommodate important guests and their entourages. The main approach to the palace was, as it still is, from the west. And the modern visitor's first impressions of the building are not so very different from those enjoyed by Wolsey's guests. The moat, having been filled in during the intervening years, has been re-dug along the front of the palace. It was the Cardinal who built the imposing gatehouse (which survives in a slightly truncated form), its deep red brickwork patterned with diamonds of blue-black. He graced it with a huge oriel window. Beyond the gatehouse opened up a pair of linked courtyards, the Base Court and the Inner Court. The first of these has remained largely unchanged, giving a vivid sense of Tudor grandeur. The courtyard presents a pleasing array of residential apartments, of red-brick and stone-mullioned windows, of fancy chimneys (restored by the Victorians) and lead-capped turrets, much as Wolsey would have known.

Part of Wolsey's Great Kitchen.

Beyond the Base Court, however, rather more has changed. Around his second courtyard Wolsey laid out the more important buildings of the palace. As the northern edge of the courtyard he either retained or rebuilt Daubeney's Great Hall. It was the place where he and his retainers could both eat and play. To feed his court, Wolsey created vast brick-built kitchens just to the north of the hall, together with a range of timber kitchen offices; and beyond them, on the plot of land still within the boundary of the moat, he planted his orchards and vegetable gardens. Of these various elements only the kitchens and the orchards survive, at least in part.

Along the east range of the second courtyard Wolsey constructed a three-storey 'stacked lodging' to provide permanent suites of rooms for the King and Queen, and for their daughter, Princess Mary. This vertical arrangement, with the three floors linked by a grand processional stair, was regarded as the acme of architectural sophistication. Henry VII had used a similar scheme at Richmond. It was derived from the example of contemporary French and Burgundian models. The King's rooms ran along the first floor, the Queen's were on the second, and Princess Mary's were on the ground floor. The King's suite had four principal rooms and a Bedchamber for greater privacy. The Queen, on the floor above, had only two State rooms and her Bedchamber.

Wolsey, it seems, at first used the rooms in Daubeney's existing range, which made up the southern boundary of the courtyard. In the mid 1520s, however, he demolished the building and increased the size of the courtyard, establishing a new south range roughly in line with the present alignment. And it was there that he then made his own lodgings. It seems probable, though, that on important state occasions the Cardinal would have used the public rooms in the King's suite.

For his recreation and exercise Wolsey built a long two-storey gallery as an extension of the south side of the palace. It ran eastwards, out towards the park, while beyond the second courtyard on the northern side of the site he constructed a new Chapel. It was in the sheltered space between these two 'arms' that Wolsey created his Knot Garden as a place of retreat and contemplation. George Cavendish, who was Wolsey's gentleman-usher and biographer, was moved to verse when describing the scene, with its intricately planted box hedges framing beds of herbs and flowers:

My gardens sweet, enclosed with walles strong
Embanked with benches to sytt and take my rest,
The knots so enknotted, it cannot be exprest;
With arbors and ayles so pleasant and so dulce,
The pestylent airs with flavours to repulse.

The Knot Garden that now exists at Hampton Court close, though not a direct descendant of Wolsey's original, being sited on the south (rather than the east) front, is at least a homage to it. It was planted in 1924 by Ernest Law, the great historian of the palace; it is closely based on recorded Tudor designs.

Wolsey embellished his palace with the latest in European art. For the first courtyard he commissioned the Florentine sculptor, Giovanni de Maiano, to make a series of terracotta medallion-busts of the Roman Emperors to adorn the turrets on each side of the gateway to the inner courtyard. They were amongst the first works of Renaissance art seen in Britain, and are still to be seen on the walls of the palace. Above the gateway leading through into the second courtyard he fixed his own coat of arms, framed with pillars, supported by two cherubs and surmounted by the Cardinal's hat of which he was so proud.

In all but the servants' quarters there was a riot of decoration and conspicuous consumption. No surface was left undecorated: tapestries were hung over linenfold panelling; painted friezes ran up to carved cornices; ceilings were moulded, gilded and painted; tables and windowsills were laid with rich carpets (in an effort to curry favour, the Venetian ambassador presented Wolsey with a consignment of sixty carpets from Damascus); cupboards were decked with splendid arrays of plate. Canopies of cloth of gold were suspended above Wolsey's chairs. Even the rush-strewn floors were scented with saffron.

All the beds (280 were kept ready for guests at all times) were provided with rich hangings and covers. The Cardinal's own four-poster was a luxurious affair piled with soft wool mattresses, fine white blankets trimmed with 'lamb's fur',

quilts of sarcenet paned white and green, and embroidered with his coat of arms and the image of the Crown of Thorns. His pillow cases – in a design which seems to prefigure Gianni Versace – were seamed with black silk and decorated with gold fleurs-de-lys. The walls of the Bedchamber were hung with a set of tapestries depicting the Seven Deadly Sins.

Although most of Wolsey's chambers have been destroyed, one set of early-sixteenth-century rooms survives in the southwest corner of Clock Court. They are thought to have been the Cardinal's private apartments. Their interiors have been

The Knot Garden was designed by the historian Ernest Law as a homage to Wolsey's.

ABOVE *One of Giovanni de Maiano's terracotta roundels.* ABOVE RIGHT *Wolsey's coat of arms.*

much altered and restored but some features survive. The linenfold panelling and the simple stone fireplaces are probably original. The ribbed ceiling in one of the rooms is decorated with the motif of the Cardinal's badge. An even stronger hint of the character of Wolsey's palace can be gleaned from the small room known as the Wolsey Closet in the east range of Clock Court. Although largely a Victorian reconstruction, its richly gilded ornamental ceiling and cornice, its frieze of High Renaissance paintings, and its deeply carved panelling provide an authentic taste of early-sixteenth-century opulence.

All the splendour had a purpose. When Wolsey was criticized for his extravagance he retorted, 'How think ye? Were it better for me, being in the honour and dignity I am, to coin my pillars and my pole-axes and give the money to five or six beggars? Do you reckon the Commonwealth better than five or six beggars?'

Wolsey's establishment at Hampton Court was the image of the King's. And the life he led there reflected the protocols of court life. Besides an enormous general staff, Wolsey also had his own personal staff: a High Chamberlain and Vice-chamberlain together with twenty gentlemen-ushers, forty gentlemen cup-bearers, forty-six yeomen of his chamber 'daily to attend on his person', four counsellors 'learned in the law', sixteen doctors and a flock of secretaries and 'running footmen' to carry out his immediate commands.

FULL-BLOWN DIGNITY

Although Hampton Court had been conceived as a place of leisure it was near enough to London to allow Wolsey to transact business from it. Ambassadors and petitioners would seek him out. His mornings were almost always given over to audiences, his afternoons to correspondence and counsel. Nevertheless, when the day's business was done there was time for revelling.

The magnificence of Wolsey's life at Hampton Court seemed to some observers to rival – if not surpass – the King's. The poet, John Skelton, in one of his many satires upon the Cardinal, asked:

Why come ye not to Court?
To which Court?
To the Kynges Courte,
Or to Hampton Court?
But Hampton Court
Hath the preemynence...

Henry himself, at this stage, seems to have been content to enjoy the amenities provided by his chief adviser. He visited Hampton Court often. George Cavendish records one particularly memorable occasion when Henry and a party of masked revellers arrived at Hampton Court pretending to be emissaries from a foreign court. Wolsey was hosting 'a solemn banquet in the Chamber of Presence', but he welcomed the unexpected arrivals to the feast and then urged them to take part in the evening's diversions, which seems to have included dancing, dicing and blind-man's-buff.

Wolsey – who had clearly been tipped off about the whole charade – then announced that he suspected that one of the masked revellers was in fact the King. He proposed to guess which one. His choice, however, fell on Sir Edward Neville, much to the delight and amusement of the King, who promptly revealed himself. This was the sign for fresh amusements. The tables were re-laid and then, with the King taking Wolsey's place under the 'cloth of estate', a sumptuous supper was served with 'two hundred divers dishes of wondrous costly

The Wolsey Closet: although a nineteenth century invention it gives an idea of Tudor opulence.

devices and subtleties'. 'Thus passed they forth the night with banqueting, dancing and other triumphant devices to the great comfort of the King and pleasant regard of the nobility there assembled.'

Despite the informality and merriment of this occasion, an undercurrent of tension had begun to creep into Wolsey's relations with his sovereign. Henry seems to have begun to resent his overmighty servant. In June 1525 he is said to have asked Wolsey why he had built for himself such a magnificent palace as Hampton Court. Wolsey, perhaps sensing a trap, is supposed to have replied: 'To show how noble a place a subject may offer to his sovereign.' It has been suggested that Henry

chose to take the remark at face value and accepted the palace as a gift. He had a new lease drawn up, transferring to him not only the palace building but also all its contents – the tapestries and pictures, the hangings, even the furniture.

Nevertheless, even after this transfer Wolsey was still allowed to continue living at the palace. It was a valuable asset as a setting for his state business. Entertainment, though it offered some moments of private diversion, also had its political uses. Hampton Court was an ideal setting to impress ambassadors.

In 1527, when Henry and Wolsey were seeking to cement an alliance with France by betrothing the ten-year-old Princess Mary to the thirty-three-year-old King of France, Francis I, they celebrated the arrangement with a grand reception at Hampton Court for the French diplomatic mission led by Duc Anne de Montmorency. The reception was hosted by Cardinal Wolsey.

Cavendish gives a wonderfully vivid account of the preparations.

My Lord Cardinal called before him his principal officers – his steward, treasurer, comptroller, and the clerks of his kitchen – whom he commanded neither to spare for any costs, expenses or travail, to make them such a triumphant banquet as they may not only wonder at here but also make a glorious report thereof in their country to the great honour of the King and his realm... They sent forth all the caterers, purveyors, and divers persons to prepare of the finest viands that they could get either for money or friendship among my Lord's friends. Also they sent for all the expertest cooks and cunning persons in the art of cookery which were within London

or that might be gotten elsewhere to beautify this noble feast... The cooks wrought both night and day in subtleties and many crafty devices; where lacked neither gold, silver, nor any costly thing meet for the purpose.

No detail of preparation was overlooked. Armies of carpenters, joiners and masons were brought in to repair and make good. 'The yeomen and grooms of the wardrobes were busied hanging of the chambers with costly hangings, and furnishing the same with beds of silk and other furniture for the same in every degree.'

It was a tight schedule, perhaps too tight. The French guests arrived 'before the hour of their appointment' and had to be taken off to the nearby park at Hanworth for a day's hunting. They arrived back at Hampton Court at dusk and were shown to their various chambers where great fires had been lit and wine and bread had been set out for their refreshment until the time for supper. The most important members of the party – the Duc de Montmorency and his retinue of 'the noblest gentlemen in France' – dined in the Chamber of Presence 'wherein was a gorgeous and precious cloth of estate hanged up replenished with many goodly gentlemen ready to serve'.

Wolsey, with a calculated demonstration of preoccupation, did not appear himself until after the first course had been cleared away. He arrived, moreover, dressed in his riding rig. The whole party rose at his entrance.

Then the second course was brought in. It was, claims Cavendish, a spread such that 'the Frenchmen never saw the like'. It is easy to believe him. The food was fashioned into a host of curious and ingenious shapes: 'There were beasts, birds, fowls of divers kinds, and personages, most lively made and conterfeit in dishes; some fighting, as it were, with swords, some with guns and crossbows; some vaulting and leaping; some dancing with ladies, some on horses in complete harness, jousting with long and sharp spears and with many more devices.' One of the French party was a noted chess-player and Wolsey had had his cooks create a cake in the form of a chess set; he presented it to the man, ordering that a special case be made so that he could ship the whole thing back to France intact. A succession of toasts were then drunk. By the end of the banquet, the Frenchmen had consumed so much that they had to be helped to their beds.

Although the party was accounted a great success it was the last that Wolsey hosted at Hampton Court. Relations between the Cardinal and the King were deteriorating fast.

For some years Henry had been wanting to divorce Catherine of Aragon. It was not that he disliked her but he needed an heir, and his Queen, despite a succession of pregnancies, had succeeded in presenting him with only a single living daughter. In 1525 Catherine was forty, and her childbearing days were over. Henry, meanwhile, had developed a consuming passion for Anne Boleyn, a young lady of the court, who refused to yield to his demands without the assurance of marriage. The Pope's sanction was necessary to grant a divorce, and Wolsey was entrusted with the task of arranging the matter.

He adopted a plausible – if spurious – line of approach: Catherine had been married to Henry's older brother, Arthur, before his untimely death. Although a papal dispensation had been granted allowing Henry to marry his brother's widow, Wolsey now claimed that it was invalid and the marriage must be terminated at once. Pope

Catherine of Aragon.

Clement VII showed himself willing to accept this line of reasoning and there seems little doubt that the divorce would have gone through, but for events on the Continent. A war between France and the Holy Roman Emperor, Charles V, culminated in defeat of the French forces and the capture of Clement VII by the Emperor. Charles was the nephew of Catherine of Aragon and he was adamant that no divorce should be granted to her husband.

Henry lost patience with Wolsey, who backed France in the ensuing European conflict. He decided to take up the reins of government himself – and to take up the palace at Hampton Court too. Wolsey was stripped of all his offices, except his archepiscopacy, and banished to York.

TEXTILES AND TAPESTRY

*T*he tapestries of Hampton Court have been a source of wonder since the time of Cardinal Wolsey. The Cardinal had a consuming passion for the stuff. He had agents constantly at work for him, scouring the markets and monitoring the workshops of Flanders and beyond. Sir Richard Gresham was one of his buyers. He measured up the chambers at Hampton Court before travelling to northern France in 1522. In just one month he bought twenty-one complete sets – over 130 pieces. Such bulk purchases were not uncommon. There were a lot of rooms at Hampton Court, and in the important chambers the tapestries were changed regularly according to the importance of an occasion.

Although Wolsey bought many sets decorated with biblical scenes he also acquired numerous tapestries illustrating mythological, literary and rustic subjects. He customized many of his tapestries by having them framed with 'new borders of my lord cardinal's arms'. Others had borders sewn 'with the arms of England and Spain, with roses and daisies', in honour of King Henry VIII and Catherine of Aragon.

From Henry VIII onwards many of the monarchs who resided at Hampton Court added to Wolsey's collection. It was Henry himself who bought the exquisite nine-piece set of 'The History of Abraham', after designs by Bernard van Orley. These were – and still are – regarded

Tapestry conservation still requires patience and skill.

as being amongst the greatest treasures in the palace. At the sale of Charles I's possessions they were valued at £8,000, while Raphael's cartoons were marked at £300.

Care of such valuable artefacts was always a matter of serious concern. The tapestries were under the charge of the Master of the King's Great Wardrobe. Regular repairs were undertaken. As early as 1524 there is an account of seven pieces of tapestry to be 'shorne and new dressed on the wrong side, and made mete for the hanging of the halle at Hampton Court'. And substantial work was carried out by William III when he creamed the collection to decorate his new apartments. The Abraham series, together with some forty other pieces, were thoroughly 'cleaned and mended', worn areas were rewoven and new selvages were added to the tapestries.

Cleaning was a curious process, as Robert Allen, a tapestry conservation expert, explains: 'Although there might have been some attempt at wet cleaning, most cleaning work was carried out with bread. They used bread almost as one would use a rubber on paper. The glutinous nature of the bread would pick up all sorts of dirt off the tapestry, and then the surface would be lightly brushed to clear the crumbs.' Nevertheless, the system was far from ideal; some bread always remained on the tapestry. It was a time-consuming process. After his round of cleaning and mending, John Vanderbank, the King's Yeoman arras mender, was able to put in a hefty bill of £206 12s 9d for all the work he had undertaken.

Nowadays the 'arras mending' and cleaning are done by the Textile Conservation Studio which, very conveniently, is based at Hampton Court, in rooms on Tennis Court Lane. The studio was established at the beginning of the century by Morris & Co., the firm founded by William Morris which had done so much to revive an interest in tapestry as an art form. Since the 1970s, as Robert Allen explains, 'the emphasis of the studio has shifted from restoration to conservation'. It has rapidly developed into the country's leading resource for such work. Tapestries and textiles from all the royal palaces, as well as from other public and private collections, are sent to Hampton Court for cleaning and conservation.

The difference between restoration and conservation is subtle. 'Conservation,' explains Lynsay Shephard, one of the conservators, 'is geared towards guaranteeing the long-term survival of objects, stabilizing them chemically sometimes, reinforcing splits. But restoration – and this is specific to textiles, I think – often tends to be a case of faking a good condition, putting back missing

The tapestries are stretched on specially designed looms during the conservation process.

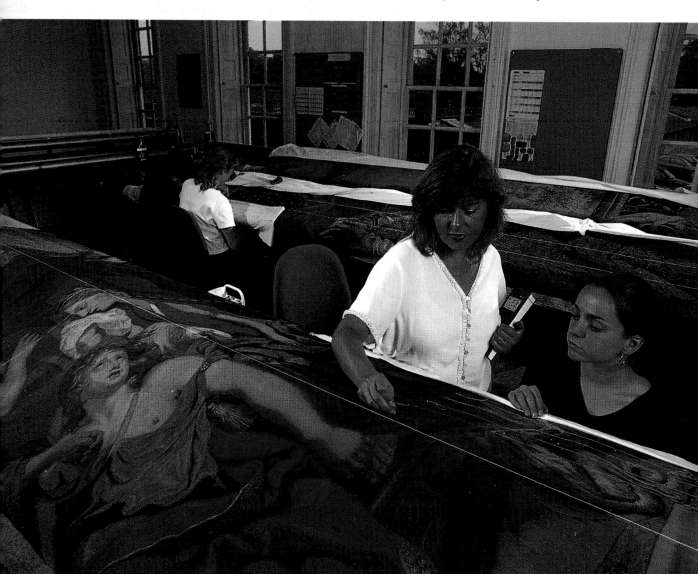

areas. It is almost always detrimental to the condition and the value of a textile in the long term.'

'Tapestries may look sturdy,' says Jenny Band, the studio's Director, 'but they have all sorts of molecular weaknesses. In a tapestry everything is in a state of mutability and entropy – the threads, the dyes, the weave. We are mediators, trying to slow down the process of decay.'

Jenny isolates several 'risk' areas affecting tapestries: 'inexpert handling', fluctuating humidity levels, damage from light and the build-up of acidity levels in the actual textiles. 'People who come into the studio and see us working away at tapestries on our special looms tend to think that conservation work is a serene, domestic activity, but in fact it is a very technical business. It requires a wide range of knowledge: organic chemistry, physics and art history are all important parts of our discipline. As well as the loom room, we also have a laboratory.'

Although the studio carries out much work on the tapestries themselves – reinforcing weak areas of the weave with neutral-coloured thread and putting linen support panels on to the back of old pieces – it also provides expert advice on displaying the work in the best and safest way. The tapestries in the Great Hall used to be stretched taut on boards. Now they are top-hung – as they used to be in Tudor times – but from a Velcro strip and not from hooks and eyes, which placed uneven and undue stress on the tapestry. A computer analysis of the loading and stress revealed that the new system was 'very, very good'.

Amongst the studio's greatest assets is its unique cleaning system. A specially equipped wash building has been established on the old 'melon ground' immediately to the north of the palace. Even very large tapestries can be washed in the vast

Robert Allen at work.

tank there. It is a delicate and carefully controlled process. 'We use purified, de-ionized water,' explains Jenny. 'It is a good solvent for dirt, and allows us to monitor the pH values during the process. But it does take a couple of days to process enough water to fill the tank.'

The tapestry is unrolled on to a very flat mesh-grid and lowered into the water. A spray boom travels over the tapestry delivering detergent, with enough pressure to remove dirt. The dirt and the detergent are then taken off the surface of the tank by top-drains, before the tapestry is rinsed with clean water. During this rinsing operation the water is monitored with an ultraviolet spectrometer allowing the conservators to check that it is clear of all the detergent. 'A lot of the tapestries we receive for cleaning are still full of old soap – or soapwort,' says Jenny. 'They can sometimes lather up like giant Brillo pads when we put them in water.'

Jenny Band in her office.

Although the cleaning process is carefully controlled it still demands great care. Most of the pieces dealt with by the studio are all but priceless. And, as Jenny Band points out, 'If anything were to go wrong the chances are that the tapestry would be part of a set, so the consequence would be amplified. It might also belong to a specific room. Thus a whole scheme of decoration could be compromised.'

'There would be very, very few occasions,' Jenny admits, 'when we'll renew something. There are specific cases, such as the loss of a black outline in

The studio's system makes certain that all soap is removed while ensuring that the 'wet phase is as short as possible'. The tank is then drained and the mesh-grid is raised to allow the natural circulation of air to dry the tapestry. Heat is never applied.

The system – which has been developed specially by the studio – is regarded as the best in the world. Certainly it is a marked improvement on the previous arrangement when wet cleaning took place in a temporary tank erected outside in one of the courtyards. 'The beauty of the new system,' enthuses Robert, 'is that it involves no mechanical action or manhandling by us while the tapestry is wet. Wet wool is very much weaker than dry wool, and having to hoist a large tapestry out of a water tank while it is still wet is a very delicate operation. Now we don't have to touch the tapestry until it is dry again.'

The work, moreover, can be undertaken by one or two people, rather than by a team of ten. 'There is a great saving on labour costs,' says Jenny, 'and as we have to run as a business such considerations are important.'

a tapestry, when we would seriously consider a renewal but it would be as a recognizable conservation process. Black outlines in medieval tapestries are often lost because of the effects of iron mordants on the wool, and their loss radically affects how we perceive the composition and the character of a medieval textile. So if you don't replace the outline you are not conserving the original character of the piece.'

Nevertheless, in line with the international code of conservators, any such replacement work has to be both identifiable and reversible.

The work of the studio is complemented by the Textile Conservation Centre, one of the several independent craft organizations that has premises at Hampton Court. The centre not only carries out its own conservation work but also teaches conservation techniques, ensuring that there will be a next generation of 'arras menders' ready to work in the studio.

One of a series of tapestries depicting the life and triumphs of Alexander the Great, made from designs by Charles le Brun.

CHAPTER 2

A ROYAL PALACE

With Wolsey's fall, Henry came into possession of all the Cardinal's houses. There were five: Hampton Court, The More, York Place in London, Tyttenhanger and Esher. Of these, York Place and Hampton Court touched his imagination most keenly. Under his direction they evolved into two of the most magnificent royal palaces in England. The former he expanded and improved as his palace of Whitehall, the second he remodelled and embellished as a resort of ease and splendour. Although by the end of his reign Henry possessed more than sixty houses, Hampton Court ranked high amongst them; it was his fourth favourite, behind the palaces of Whitehall and Greenwich, and the castle at Windsor.

Henry, extreme in all his appetites, was an almost compulsive builder and refurbisher. He never took over a house without seeking to alter

and improve it. And at Hampton Court his desire to make the place perfect gave him little rest. For ten years the scaffolding was never down. There was always some fresh scheme in progress. In the decade-and-a-half between 1530 and 1546 he spent a staggering £62,000 on his work at Hampton Court, almost £20 million at today's values.

When Henry took over the palace from his disgraced minister there was work already in progress. He merely co-opted the workmen and redirected them. He wished to make his own mark upon the building. It was an assertion of independence. Wolsey, up till then, had acted as Henry's principal architectural adviser. The King now took matters into his own hands.

Henry wasted no time in setting up his own coat of arms, and his own heraldic symbols – the King's Beasts – on every available surface. In tandem with these important (if cosmetic) alterations, Henry launched into his building programme. The first phase of 'improvements' was put in train right

OPPOSITE The Great Hall, looking toward the Minstrels Gallery. ABOVE One of the King's Beasts.

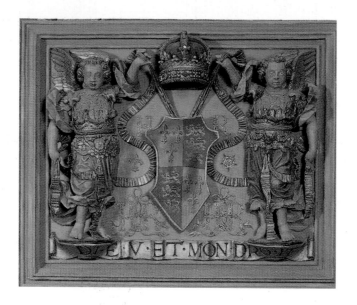

Henry VIII's arms outside the Chapel Royal.

away. It provides a revealing insight into Henry's interests and ambitions in the years around 1530, when he was emerging from the shadows of Wolsey's tutelage.

He was content, for the time being, to live on in the 'stacked lodging' created for him by Wolsey on the east side of the second courtyard; but other areas needed immediate attention. There were five elements to Henry's initial building programme: for private use he constructed a 'Bayne Tower' (to house his bathroom, and his personal apartments) and a new gallery; for recreation he built a tennis court and a bowling alley; for affairs of state he constructed a Council Chamber; to impress visitors he rebuilt or, at least, extended the Great Hall; and to feed his court he greatly enlarged the palace kitchens. Some of this work survives to this day.

Henry's Bayne Tower, although slightly remodelled in the nineteenth century, still stands in a small courtyard, not open to the public, beyond the southeast corner of the Clock Court. In form it

is a rather squat, three-storey 'donjon', attached to the main range of the court; it is now a private residence for a member of the palace workforce.

Henry built it as a sort of private wing: the ground floor housed the offices of the Privy Chamber (the Household department concerned with the King's private needs), together with a strongroom for his treasure. On the first floor were the King's private Bedchamber, his bathroom and his study, and above them were his library and jewel house. It was a place to which he could retreat away from the cares and demands of the court. And it was from the Bayne Tower that Henry gained access to the new gallery which he constructed as a second-floor addition above Wolsey's existing two-storey gallery. Although it was originally designated as a gallery for the Queen, and was – after all – situated on a level with the Queen's Apartments, there was no access to it from her suite. The arrangement served as a telling sign of the King's growing estrangement from his Queen, Catherine of Aragon. It also provided Henry with a place for private recreation and exercise.

This desire for personal privacy was a relatively modern notion. And Henry ensured that the details and decoration of his private retreats were similarly up-to-date. But the actual form of his private apartments – the donjon tower – was thoroughly medieval. Indeed Henry's Bayne Tower has the dubious distinction of being the last 'donjon' built at an English royal residence. Almost as soon as it was completed Henry seems to have sensed that it was outmoded. Within a few years he would abandon it and devise a new set of private apartments.

Privacy was not the only modern fad that Henry embraced. He was a great believer in sport, not merely as a preparation for war but as a promoter of health. Over the course of his reign he developed what almost amounted to a sports complex at Hampton Court. Henry built a new, covered 'tennis play' as an addition to Wolsey's existing open tennis court. He also constructed bowling alleys: by the end of his reign there were three at the palace – one running out to the north of the little Chapel Court, and two more down by the river. They were long, narrow, brick buildings, 20 feet wide and over 200 feet long. They provided a slightly less energetic alternative to the rigours of the tennis court.

Not all Henry's alterations at Hampton Court were for his personal benefit and pleasure. When the King was in residence, Hampton Court became the centre of government; a Council Chamber was necessary. He had one built, just to the north of his Holyday Closet. Tudor kingship, however, was as much about pomp as it was about counsel. Henry was keen to impose a sense of regal magnificence upon the palace. It was probably this that prompted him to rebuild the Great Hall.

Henry VIII's Bayne Tower as it is today.

The Hall had been the traditional setting for much of court life throughout the previous centuries, and it was still a focus for many courtly activities. Times and habits, however, were changing. Increasingly the activities taking place in the Great Hall tended to be menial or transient. Only the common servants and the lesser officials now dined in the Hall on a daily basis. As the largest covered space in the palace, the Hall had also become the setting for court revels – masques and dances. To accommodate this function there was usually a gallery at one end for minstrels, and a dais at the other on which the King could sit to watch the fun.

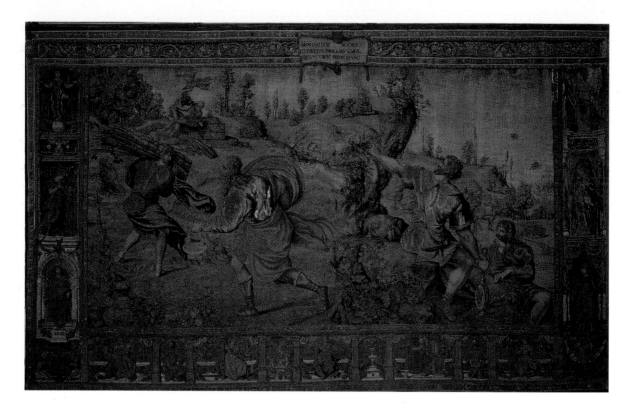

A tapestry from the Story of Abraham series.

King Henry, however, seems to have chosen to ignore the general decline in the Great Hall's importance. The same architectural conservatism that had prompted him to build his private chambers in a donjon persuaded him that he needed to have an impressive Great Hall. The exact extent of Wolsey's Hall is unknown but it, was not, Henry considered, impressive enough. He replaced it with something altogether grander and more splendid. It was the only Great Hall he built, and it was great indeed: 106 feet long, 40 feet wide and rising to 60 feet in height.

The ceiling was a magnificent hammer-beam construction designed by the King's master-carpenter James Nedeham, its surface ornately carved with grotesque heads and royal coats of arms. The whole was painted and gilded – a riot of red, blue and gold. In the middle of the roof was a three-tiered louvred vent to take out the smoke that rose from a hearth in the middle of the Hall floor. (Both the hearth and the vent have been removed, but the Hall remains, and a brass plaque on its floor indicates the position of the fire.) Henry was so eager to see the work completed that he paid the builders overtime to work into the night, providing them with an additional allowance of tallow candles for the job.

Although Henry might be considered old-fashioned in building such a Hall, several of its features were innovative. It was set not at ground level, but on the first floor. The space underneath became a gigantic cellar. The Hall was approached by a grand staircase and led on into the Great Watching Chamber, the first of the State

Apartments. It thus became, in effect, the entrance hall into the King's domain, a dazzling foretaste of royal magnificence.

It still has that impact. Although the room was heavily restored in the 1840s – a carved polychrome cornice being added, and the long-vanished Tudor glass replaced with an imposing stained-glass window depicting Henry VIII together with the pedigrees of his six wives and three children – the scale and grandeur of the space are as Henry intended. On the walls Henry hung a series of Flemish tapestries, depicting the story of Abraham, which was almost certainly commissioned specially for the space. They are still *in situ*.

Henry's other great construction project during his first years at Hampton Court was the rebuilding and extension of the kitchen block to the north of the Great Hall.

'STIR AND BUSTLE' – THE PALACE KITCHENS

Well preserved and imaginatively restored, The kitchens at Hampton Court offer a unique and vivid glimpse into the working life of the Tudor court.

Although when Henry VIII took over Hampton Court he inherited the very sizeable kitchens that Wolsey had built, he at once realized that they were not extensive enough for his household's prodigious needs. The royal household was rarely less than 800; in the winter months it could number well over a thousand. All these people had to be provided with two hot meals a day. To locate, purchase, prepare, cook, serve and clear such quantities of food was a major logistical

The butchery in the boiling house.

challenge. It was a challenge, moreover, that was constrained by two sometimes conflicting demands: the need for strict economy and the desire for imposing courtly magnificence.

For administrative purposes the household was divided into two departments: the Hall, which included all the servants, lower officials and visitors; and the Chamber, which comprised the royal family, its guests, advisers and retainers. The former was under the control of the Lord Steward (or, as he was known from 1540 onwards, the Great Master); the latter came under the supervision of the Lord Chamberlain.

The Lord Steward ruled over the service areas of any palace where the King was staying, the Chamberlain over those public chambers where the King appeared before the world. The Great Kitchen at Hampton Court would have been within the Lord Steward's sphere. The third great

Food was dressed with great elaboration.

officer of the household was the Master of the Horse. He was responsible for the King's horses, carts and carriages, as well as all the royal hunting and transport arrangements. In total the domestic staff on the royal payroll numbered almost 500, and of these about half were connected to the kitchen and its various departments. There were almost a score of such specialist 'offices': the bakehouse, pantry, cellar, buttery, spicery, saucery, pastry, wafery, confectionary, scullery, laundry, boiling house, scalding house, larder, accatry (store house), poultry, ewery, squillery, woodyard, and the Great Kitchen itself, each with its serjeant, clerk and purveyor and assistants.

Although Henry recognized the necessity of increasing the size of the palace kitchens at Hampton Court, he decided not to alter their position. Wolsey's kitchen range ran along the north front of the palace, and there was a certain virtue in the arrangement: the food-storage areas received little direct sunlight and remained cool.

Henry used the existing structure, but extended and augmented it. The size of the Great Kitchen itself was almost doubled. Much new work was also undertaken. The building scheme took almost four years to complete. Henry's new design was a well-ordered and streamlined affair: a series of small courtyards, containing storage and preparation areas, led up to the Great Kitchen chamber, as though along a straight avenue. Giving off the main kitchen-area were dressing rooms and serving hatches, so that the food could be garnished before it was despatched in due order up the stairs. The dishes were then marshalled in the space now known as the Horn Room prior to being carried through into either the newly constructed Great Hall or the Great Watching Chamber.

The structure and layout of the Hampton Court kitchen buildings – many of which survive – reveal much about how they operated. It is possible to trace the full progress of many palace supplies from their arrival on site to their appearance on the table.

The heavier items of produce tended to arrive by river. Close to the riverbank, on the open court beyond the main gatehouse, Henry built a small complex of timber-framed service-buildings. These 'Houses of Offices' (long since demolished) were designed not only for storage but also to accommodate some of the noisier, more noxious and inflammable operations of the domestic regime. They housed the woodyard where timber was delivered, cut and stored ready for use on the kitchen fires, the 'squillery' which was responsible for supplying the highly flammable rushes for the palace floors, the 'poultry' and the 'scalding house' where birds in their hundreds were first slaughtered and then plunged into boiling water to clean them and prepare them for plucking. Also there was the bakehouse – another fire risk. It was responsible for producing the court's bread. Wolsey's original bakehouse had been situated further from the palace somewhere in the Park. Henry relocated it, bringing it closer to the woodyard for fuel and the river for flour deliveries.

Moving on from the Houses of Offices, the service entrance to the palace proper was through the low gatehouse which still stands on the west front to the left of the main gateway tower. The room immediately above the service gateway housed the Counting House, the hub of domestic administrative operations. Although the Lord Steward had ultimate responsibility for such matters, much of the everyday business of administration was delegated. Beneath the Steward were three important officials: the Treasurer, Cofferer and Comptroller. They all lodged in the little courtyard inside the service gate and presided over the Office of the Greencloth. It was this office which controlled the daily expenditure of the household, paying out the wages for the entire court and monitoring the purchase and use of all supplies. It convened daily in the Counting House. The position of the Counting House was significant. It offered a commanding view of all provisions entering – or leaving – the palace kitchens.

The Horn Room where food was marshalled.

At least one of the three officers would be present there each morning, carrying a white stave as a mark of his office, and accompanied by two or three 'clerks of the greencloth'. They would seat themselves around a table spread with green baize and equipped with a counting till and a cash box. The clerks from the various kitchen departments and offices would then present themselves to have their previous day's accounts checked, to make their requests and receive their orders for the coming day. The office of the greencloth still survives as a department of the royal household. When Dennis McGuinnes, the current Deputy

Director of the palace, wished to apply for a liquor licence for the palace shops, he had to make his application to the Court of the Greencloth held at Buckingham Palace. He found them still sitting around a table covered with a green baize cloth.

Leading eastwards from the service gate towards the kitchen itself, the first courtyard housed a spicery, a chandlery (where candles were kept) and a coal cellar (as some of the kitchen stoves were coal-fired). The next yard contained the 'confectory' and the 'pastry office'. From there a passage led through to the narrow yard now known as Fish Court. Doorways led off from it into a butchery, a dry larder, a wet larder, a game larder and a boiling house. Above each of these offices the relevant clerks and officers had their lodgings.

The departments in the three outer courtyards were largely concerned with storage and the initial preparation of food. The range of produce they dealt with was relatively limited. Fruit and vegetables were available – in season – from the palace kitchen gardens and from local suppliers. Turnips, carrots, peas, beans and several varieties of cabbage were common – in both senses of the word. Turnips and beans were both denigrated as 'windy meat' by contemporary commentators. As a result vegetables played only a secondary role in the court diet.

The Tudor table was dominated by meat and fish. Both were consumed in quantity. It is estimated that in a single year the court got through more than 1,240 oxen ('beeves'), 8,200 sheep (which, as one foreign visitor noted were 'very big and fat'), 2,230 deer, 1,870 pigs, 760 calves, 53 wild boars and innumerable rabbits. Every sort of bird from the lark to the swan and even the peacock found its

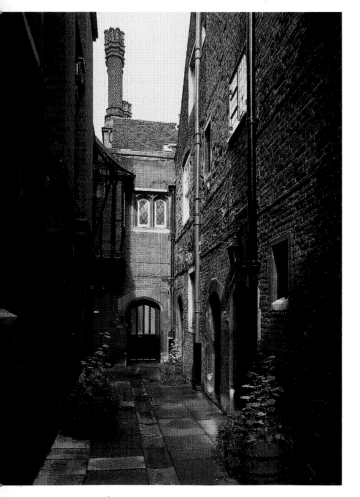

Fish Court, the hub of the palace food stores.

way – via the poultry – on to the palace menu. Hampton Court even had its own pheasant run.

The virtue of meat was that animals could be kept alive and slaughtered when required. Some cuts – such as hams – could be cured and preserved. Fish posed more problems in this respect. It was, nevertheless, a major feature of the court diet. Meat was proscribed on fast days, on important religious festivals and during Lent. Fish was eaten in its stead. In an effort to further encourage the national fishing industry Tudor governments designated not only Friday as a fast day but also Wednesday. With the aid of such legislation some 150 days in the year became fish-days.

In an era before readily available ice, fish transport and storage presented problems. Catches arrived at Hampton Court daily from the coast, layered in barrels with seaweed, and were stored in the cool of the 'wet larder'. But during the summer months even this method must have been under strain. Stocks of freshwater carp and bream were held alive in three oblong fish-ponds which Henry had dug in the area between the south-facing range of the Base Court and the river. The moat too and the river provided something towards the supply of fresh fish.

While the larders held the raw fish and meat in cool-storage, the other adjacent departments were concerned with preparing basic ingredients. The butchery skinned and jointed carcasses ready for use. The boiling house, with its vast copper cauldron set above its own furnace, boiled meat for pies and provided stock for soups. The pastry office supplied the pie covers and bases. The confectory provided marchpane (the Tudor version of marzipan), almond milk and other sweetstuffs.

Water was important for all these operations. Both the boiling house and the larder had their own

The fire in the Great Kitchen is still lit.

cisterns, and it seems probable that most of the other kitchen offices were also supplied with running water, certainly after 1540 when Henry VIII improved the palace's water-supply with the new conduit system running from Coombe Hill (see page 51). Henry also constructed – as one of his first improvements – two great 'sinks' or drains to carry off effluent 'from the kechen to Thames'. These arched brick-structures – which still run under the kitchen courts – were 14 feet high and 10 feet wide. They passed under the moat, through the outer court and into the river, thus keeping the kitchen area clean and preserving the moat from pollution.

If the raw materials were gathered and prepared in the outer courts, the actual cooking was done in the Great Kitchen itself. It was there that the ingredients were combined: the pies were made up; the haunches of meat roasted on great spits before the open fire, or boiled in cauldrons hung over the flames; the sauces simmered over the even heat of charcoal burners.

Tudor recipes were alive with interesting combinations of flavours – many of them unexpected to the modern palate. Meat and fish were often cooked or dressed with fruit. Pork was served with raisins and apples; carp was eaten with prunes; pies were stuffed with salmon and dried figs.

Many spices were used in the sauces that accompanied almost every dish. This was both a matter of taste and a wise precaution to mask the suspect freshness of the meat or fish. The spices were stored in the spicery out in the first of the service courtyards. Many of them – such as pepper, cinnamon, cloves and mace – were exotic and expensive imports from the eastern end of the Mediterranean; others, however, like mustard, were easily grown natives.

Although there were always meat or fish dishes on the menu, the basis of most meals – particularly those that were served in the Great Hall – was pottage and bread. Pottage was a Tudor staple, a rich broth made from meat-, poultry- or fish-stock drawn from the boiling-house cauldron, thickened with barley or oatmeal and flavoured with herbs. The bread served at court varied in its quality depending upon the rank of the diner. The lesser members of the court – the majority of those dining in the Great Hall – were served with bap-like loaves of 'cheat', a bread made from coarse flour. The upper courtiers ate 'manchet', which was baked with fine-grade flour.

The modern distinction between sweet and savoury dishes seems to have been only partially observed. There were pudding-style creations – flavoured custards and spiced fritters – but they were not always served at the end of the meal.

The heat and bustle of a Tudor kitchen are hard to imagine. Despite the great height of the kitchen chamber, the limited number of windows, the constant presence of three great fires, several ovens and numerous other burners must have made things very warm indeed. One visitor described them as 'veritable hells'. The spit-turners were each equipped with a jug of ale to quench their thirst.

And yet somehow, amidst all the infernal clatter, the food was prepared, and cooked, and then presented at the service hatches, ready to be taken up to the Hall.

Although much of what was produced in the kitchen was mere fuel for a hungry court, food could, on occasion, provide an opportunity for conspicuous display. Prodigy dishes became a feature of important banquets: roasted peacocks were served re-dressed in their own plumage, their beaks and feet gilded; animals, buildings and curiosities were modelled in marchpane and coloured with edible dyes. These dishes, of course, required long and elaborate preparation. Two special dressing chambers were established just off the Great Kitchen for the construction of such wonders.

Although most of the meal was brought up to the Great Hall from the kitchen, two items – bread and drink – arrived from separate sources. The bread was sent in from the bakehouse via the pantry. Beer and wine were dispensed from the cellar via the buttery. As with every other aspect of court life their use was strictly regulated according to rank and estate. While upper courtiers were entitled to wine, most of the court drank ale at mealtimes. And they drank it in enormous quantities: 600,000 gallons a year. One Spanish visitor considered that the court's daily intake would 'fill the Valladolid river'. It was watery stuff, however, much weaker than modern beer, and only mildly intoxicating.

A corner of the Great Kitchen.

Wine was more dangerous on this score, though it too was weaker than it is now. It came from France (particularly Bordeaux) and from Germany. It was often enlivened with additions. 'Hippocras', a spiced concoction of red wine, sugar, cinnamon, ginger and cardamom, heated and then strained through a muslin bag, was popular amongst the court. As one foreign observer noted, 'In summer the ladies and some gentlemen put sugar in their wine, with the result that there are great goings on at court.'

At the same time as extending the kitchen and kitchen courts, Henry also expanded Wolsey's cellars. Two new cellars were made beneath the new Great Hall. Both are still visible, restored to their original form. The larger one was for beer, the smaller – the Privy Cellar – was for the King's wine. Later a third vaulted cellar, also for wine, was added beyond the Privy Cellar. The wine was stored in barrels, and served in pitchers. The King and Queen, however, had wine bottles, which were kept in a special cupboard in the 'drinking house' attached to the cellar.

There was, in the Tudor court, a strictly defined hierarchy as to who ate what, where and when. A list was kept of all those entitled to dine at court, specifying each person's position in the scheme of things. The kitchen staff themselves were about the lowest on this list. They dined where they worked, at tables in the Great Kitchen.

The greater part of the food that they prepared went to the Great Hall where it was served to the senior servants and lesser officials of the court. The Yeomen of the Guard were amongst those who ate in the Great Hall. They dined twice a day: once at noon, and then again at about four in the afternoon. Those sitting at the long-tables in the Great Hall were served in groups – or messes – of four. Each

dish brought to the table would be designed to cater for a quartet. The mess-mates would then divide it amongst themselves. There were usually about five dishes to a meal, although on important feast days the number could almost double.

Senior officials, and courtiers with any pretensions to importance, would not dine in the Great Hall but in the Great Watching Chamber next door, while the King's closest advisers were nearer to the sovereign, in the Presence Chamber.

The King himself ate in his Privy Chamber, waited on by his gentlemen. His food was not produced from the Great Kitchen but from his own Privy Kitchen. The dishes served to the King and to the highest courtiers were both more plentiful and more elaborate. They were prepared using only the best ingredients. Special bread came from a Privy Bakehouse adjacent to the common bakehouse, and the wine came from the Privy Cellar. Although the King was sometimes obliged to entertain important guests, he ate most often in solitary splendour, or with his Queen, surrounded only by his intimates.

Henry initially took over Wolsey's Privy Kitchen, which stood directly under his private dining chamber and was connected to it by a 'vice stair'. This had the twin benefits of ensuring the food arrived hot at the royal table and warming the royal apartments with the rising heat of the kitchen ranges. When Henry expanded his lodgings in 1537 he almost replicated this arrangement, siting his new Privy Kitchen under his private rooms.

Henry's Queens were served by their own Privy Kitchens. Anne Boleyn's lodgings included a Privy Kitchen and adjoining larder underneath, and connected to, the Queen's Presence Chamber, where she dined. The virtues of proximity were, however, less apparent to the female members of the Royal Household. Queen Elizabeth found the noise and smell of the Privy Kitchen unpleasant and had it moved to a more distant position, beyond the main kitchen range. This still survives, in the less gastronomically exalted form of the Privy Kitchen Coffee Shop.

When the King chose to sup in one of the intimate banqueting houses dotting the grounds, the Privy Kitchen staff would provide the food. Many of the banqueting houses were equipped with their own little kitchens.

Every aspect of Tudor court dining – from the Royal Banqueting House to the Great Hall – was stamped with excess. This was a matter not of greed but of providence. Superfluity was an important part of the system. The courtiers would pass on their left-overs to the servants, and what the servants did not eat was given to the beggars who gathered at the gate of every great house.

Baked Carp

Take of the Scales and take forth the Gall and with Cloves, mace and salte, season it and take corans and prunes and put about the carpe and take butter and put it upon him and let him bake two hours.
[T. Dawson, *The Good Housewife's Jewell*, 1585]

Roast Pork

Take your pig and drawe it and take ixor and parboyle yt and stire yt with a little creame and yolk of egg, and put thereto grated bread, [rose]mary, small raysons, nuttmeg, pouder of mace, sugar and salt stire these together and put into the pigs belly and sewe up the pigs belly and spitt him with the haire on and when it is half enough put off the skinne and take hede for tearing of the fatt, thereon. Then bast yt well and rub on it with creame and fine bread crumbs, sugar, cinammon and ginger and let it be done browne.
[BL Sloane MS 234.b.f17]

Hippocras

Take of chosen Cinamon two ounces, of fine Ginger one ounce, of Graines half an ounce, bruse them all and stampe them in three or fower pints of good odiferous wine, with a pound of suger, by the space of foure and twentie hourse, than put them into an Ipocrasse bagge of wollen and so received the liquor. The readiest and best way is to put the spices with the halfe pounde of suger, and the wine into a bottell, or a stone potte stopped close, and after xxiiii houres it will be ready, then cast a thinne linnen cloth, or a piece of boulter clothe on the mouthe and let in so much run through as ye will occupie at once, and keepe ye vessell close, for it will so well keepe bothe the spirite, odour and vertue of the wine and the spices.
[J. Partridge, *The Treasurie of Commodious Conceits and Hidden Secrets*, 1584]

Desert and Desire

Throughout the first phase of his building work at Hampton Court, Henry was engaged in negotiating his divorce. The problem was proving intractable. Henry spent long hours pacing in his gallery with his new chancellor, Sir Thomas More, discussing the options open to him. During the summer of 1530 he summoned the leading clergy and canon lawyers to Hampton Court to discuss whether 'in virtue of the privilege possessed by the Kingdom, Parliament could and would enact that, notwithstanding the Pope's prohibition, the cause of the divorce should be decided by the Archbishop of Canterbury'. Nothing was decided at once. But after the meeting broke up, Henry called the Papal nuncio to the palace and told him that unless the Pope complied with his wishes for a divorce, he would deny the force of Papal authority in England.

As a sideshow to these negotiations, Henry decided to bring proceedings for treason against the disgraced Wolsey. The Cardinal, who had been sent up to York, was summoned to the Tower of London. He never reached the capital. He died on his way south, at Leicester. The news of his death was brought to Henry at Hampton Court by George Cavendish, Wolsey's gentleman-usher.

Cavendish found the King practising his archery in the Park. He wrote:

Perceiving him occupied in shooting, I thought it not my duty to trouble him, but leaned to a tree, intending to stand there, and to attend his gracious pleasure. Being in a great study, at the last the King came suddenly behind me where I stood, and clapped his hand upon my shoulder, and when I perceived him, I fell upon my knee. To whom he said, calling me by name, 'I will,' quoth he, 'make an end of my game, and then will I talk with you,' and so departed to his mark, whereat the game was ended.

Then the King delivered his bow unto the yeoman of his bows, and went his way inward to the palace, whom I followed; howbeit he called for Sir John Gage, with whom he talked until he came at the garden postern gate, and there entered; the gate being shut after him, which caused me to go my ways.

And being gone but a little distance, the gate was opened again, and there Sir Harry Norris called me again, commanding me to come in to the King, who stood behind the door in a nightgown of russet velvet furred with sables; before whom I kneeled down, being with him there all alone the space of an hour and more, during which time he examined me of divers weighty matters concerning my lord, wishing that liever than £20,000 that he had lived.

If Henry expressed some pang of regret at Wolsey's death it is unlikely that his sentiments were echoed by his new love, Anne Boleyn. Henry had tried to foster relations between the two. He even persuaded Anne to send the Cardinal a present of a small gold bar that Christmas. Nevertheless, a current of mutual enmity had always flowed beneath the surface of their relations. Henry had already installed Anne at Hampton Court but the frustrations of the long-delayed divorce from Catherine of Aragon began to tell.

In December 1532 it was discovered that Anne was pregnant. Henry's divorce became a matter of increased urgency. If the Pope would not comply, the break from Rome must be made, and made quickly. Even so, Henry could not wait. He married Anne secretly and illegally in January 1533. The Archbishop of Canterbury did not grant the annulment of his marriage to Catherine until May.

Anne was crowned at Westminster Abbey the following month. The royal couple then proceeded to Hampton Court for their honeymoon. The month was given over to banquets, revels and dances. The vivacious, dark-eyed Queen loved dancing and despite her pregnant condition would lead the court out on to the floor.

Anne's high spirits were coupled with a quick intelligence and a cultured mind. She had been educated in an atmosphere of humanist inquiring, and she took an interest in both art and architecture. Having safely married and crowned his new bride, Henry launched into a fresh series of building schemes in her honour. And Anne, it seems, contributed her own ideas to their form and direction.

Some of the alterations were easily achieved. Anne's coat of arms and her heraldic badge – the falcon – were conspicuously displayed throughout the palace: on pennants, plaques and vanes. They were carved on to some of the bosses being affixed to the ceiling of the Great Hall, and set in the vaulting of the gateway leading from the first to the second courtyard. Anne's initials appeared entwined in a lovers' knot with those of her husband.

But beyond these heraldic flourishes Anne and Henry initiated a complete remodelling of the royal apartments. A new suite of lodgings for the Queen was created and the King's lodgings were also comprehensively refurbished. The layout reverted to the traditional English model. Instead of the Queen's lodgings being stacked above the King's, both sets were on the same first-floor level. The Queen's new lodgings extended along the eastern boundary of the palace. They ran parallel to the King's lodgings and were connected to them not only by a small extension to the King's Long Gallery but also by a new gallery built for the Queen's use.

Anne Boleyn.

The arrangement created a new courtyard. The arcading that ran around it on the ground floor gave it its name: Cloister Green Court.

The small room at the end of the King's Long Gallery became one of the marvels of the palace, a chamber of the richest and most fantastical decoration. It soon gained the name of 'Paradise'. No sixteenth-century visitor could pass up the opportunity to inspect its marvels. As one noble traveller recounted, 'everything glitters so with silver, gold and jewels, as to dazzle one's eyes'.

Of the King's apartments, only the Great Watching Chamber, the first of the state rooms, remains, but the general layout of the suite can be established and is worth recording. It was a design

ABOVE Anne Boleyn's badge. RIGHT Her initials entwined with Henry's

scheme which – with only minor modifications – continued in royal palaces for over 200 years.

The State Apartments followed a linear and symbolic progression, each room leading closer to the King and the true seat of power. The Great Watching Chamber represented a first hurdle for those wishing to see the King. Henry rebuilt it completely, increasing it in size, in 1535. It is still an imposing room. Although some of its decorative details were removed in the seventeenth century and the stained glass in the casements is Victorian, the scale is unaltered. And within the broad high space, the ceiling with its geometric pattern of gilded battens and drop pendants, and the walls with their vast tapestries from cornice to floor, give a real idea of the stark grandeur of Henry's plan.

The outer door of the chamber was manned by 'Yeomen Ushers', officials charged with 'not permitting or suffering any person to enter, but such as by his discretion shall be sure good and mete for the place'. It was a broad remit. Should there be any trouble, the ushers were supported by the Yeomen of the Guard, who were stationed in the room. This personal royal bodyguard of hand-picked men (they were usually chosen for their height and bearing) had been instituted by Henry VIII. They were clad in the red habits familiar to anyone who has visited the Tower of London and seen their contemporary descendants. They kept watch in the chamber at all times, giving the room its name, and projecting an aura of military might which must have impressed those who entered. To ensure that the guards on duty never had to desert their posts, they were provided with a small 'garderobe' – or lavatory – just off the chamber itself.

Despite its primary functions as a guard-room and ante-chamber, the Great Watching Chamber was also used as a dining-room for senior courtiers. At night it became a dormitory for the pages and other junior chamber-staff.

The general upkeep of the room, as of all the State Apartments to which the court had access, was the work of the pages. They – rather like the palace housekeepers of today – were required to 'dress, repair, and make clean' the rooms. They also had to wait upon the gathered courtiers. Leading off the Great Watching Chamber was a small room – the Pages' Chamber – where they awaited instructions and ate. Each of the State Apartments would have had its own Pages' Chamber. The room also provided a useful dressing place where courtiers who were due to be presented to the King could be helped into their ceremonial robes by the pages. It was in the Pages' Chamber off the Great Watching Chamber that Catherine Parr's brother and uncle were prepared before they were ennobled by the King in 1546.

The actual ennobling ceremony took place in the room beyond the Great Watching Chamber, the Presence Chamber. Here the King would sit on a raised dais under a 'cloth of estate' – a canopy of cloth of gold. From this exalted position he would receive foreign embassies, ennoble favoured courtiers or even, upon rare occasions, dine in the presence of his courtiers. The tapestries, friezes and ceiling decorations were all more sumptuous than those in the Great Watching Chamber. The

The Great Watching Chamber: the ceiling incorporates the badges of Henry VIII and Jane Seymour.

The Pages' Chamber

Presence Chamber was the ceremonial hub of the palace. It was where the King projected his full majesty out on to the world and the court.

In the early Tudor period access to the Presence Chamber had been very restricted, but during the course of Henry's reign it became more open. The room, as a result, began to get more crowded, as more courtiers were granted admission. Henry's initial response was to use the Presence Chamber less. He retreated into his Privy Chamber, transferring to it functions that had once belonged to the Presence Chamber.

The Privy Chamber marked the beginning of the King's 'inward' lodgings. Between the 'outward' and 'inward' chambers there was a short passageway, a sort of architectural safety-valve. In this brief passage were two small closets connected by a window-hatch. One housed a tiny altar, the other a 'kneeling place' for the King. It was an arrangement that allowed the King to hear his daily Mass in private. The King could emerge from his Privy Chamber at the appropriate hour; his personal chaplains could come and go – without having to pass either through the outward or the inward chambers – via a little staircase that led up into the connecting passageway.

Very few courtiers were admitted to the inner sanctum of the Privy Chamber. It was where the King gathered about him his intimate advisers and friends, and it was where he dined. The running of the Privy Chamber, and of all the inward lodgings, was the responsibility of the Groom of the Stool. Under him were ranged the Gentlemen of the Chamber, or 'gentilhommes de chambre' as they were styled to give them a gloss of French sophistication. These courtiers were well-born young favourites of the King's. There were at all times at least two of them in attendance on the King. At night they slept in the Privy Chamber itself.

Serving not only the King but also the Gentlemen of the Chamber there were grooms, ushers and pages. Also attached to the Privy Chamber staff was a barber, whose duty it was to shave the King each day. Musicians were often in attendance to entertain the King and his companions.

Beyond the Privy Chamber lay the King's Bedchamber and beyond that his 'secret places' – his private bedroom, study, bathroom and garderobe, housed (as we have seen) in the Bayne Tower which he had constructed. Only the Groom of the Stool had official right of entry to these private rooms. Indeed the official's very title derived from his duty of attending to the King upon his close-stool, or lavatory.

While many of the garderobes in the courtier lodgings were connected to a sewerage system which funnelled into the main palace drains, the King's close-stool was little more than a glorified chamber-pot. It consisted of a wooden chest with a hole in the lid, and a pewter pot within. The chest might be covered in rich velvets and trimmed with ribbon in an attempt to lend it a regal air, but the pewter pot still had to be emptied by hand. This was the duty of the Groom of the Stool, or 'Stole'. He also had to provide the King with a piece of linen or flannel with which he might 'wipe his nether end'.

Given the unbalanced nature of the Tudor royal diet, with its heavy emphasis on meat and sauce to the exclusion of almost all fruit and vegetables, the condition of the royal bowels was a matter of constant concern. An account survives by Sir Thomas Heneage, who was Groom of the Stole in the late 1530s, of a nocturnal visit to the garderobe, paid by the King after he had been dosed with a laxative pill and a 'clyster'. '[He] slept unto two of the clock in the morning and then his grace rose to go to the stole, which by working of the pills and glyster that his highness had taken before, had a very fair siege.'

Although detailed evidence is scarce, it seems that the arrangement and management of Anne Boleyn's new lodgings echoed those of the King's, although her 'secret places' were laid out, not in a donjon, but all on the same level as her Privy Chamber. It was probably to the Queen's Bedchamber that the King went when he wished to sleep with her, reaching her lodgings via the connecting gallery.

Close to the angle of the King's Gallery and the Queen's Lodgings, a Privy Stair was made. It provided the royal couple with shared access to a new Privy Garden that had been established on the south side, in the angle between the palace and the Thames. It was a special preserve for the King and Queen, walled off from the rest of the grounds.

Tudor ideas about garden design were rather different from those of today. The main rectangle of the garden area was divided into about twenty enclosures with wooden posts and rails all painted in alternating stripes of white and green. A German visitor during the reign of Elizabeth I described the ground within these enclosures as 'very much resembling a chessboard', with the earth divided up in 'square cavities', some of which were 'filled with red brick-dust, some with white sand and some with green lawn'. And in the middle of each 'chessboard' was a brass sundial. Only around the edges were flowers planted. The surviving records mention violets, primroses, roses, mint, sweet williams, 'gilliflowers' and other 'sweet flowers'; they also mention payment for 'weeders'.

At the end of the garden and separated from it by a brick wall was a triangular plot on which Henry created his Mount Garden. This seems to have been a rather less formal and more fantastical place than the Privy Garden proper. The aforementioned German visitor was much impressed by the extraordinary topiary he found there: 'There were all manner of shapes, men and women, centaurs, sirens, serving maids with baskets, French lilies [fleurs-de-lys] and delicate crenellations' all made from box, rosemary and other evergreens.

The garden was dominated by a large conical mound, spiralled like a snail's shell. Although founded upon a large brick substructure, its sides were turfed and planted with rosemary bushes, woodbine, hawthorns, pear trees and other shrubs. Also lining the spiralled ascent were a succession of striped poles set with the 'Kynges and Quenys beestes in tymber'. And at the summit was a magnificent circular banqueting house, set with numerous windows, giving views out across the river, the park and the gardens. The roof was capped with a lead dome.

This Great Round Arbour as it was called, was only the most spectacular of several banqueting houses and gazebos dotting the palace grounds. Each of the three corners of the Mount Garden wall was graced with a little crenellated banqueting tower.

Breaching the far wall of the Mount Garden was the covered 'Water Gallery'. This was a curious structure, with rooms, battlements and oriel windows, which ran down to the royal mooring place on the river. It provided a suitably magnificent point of arrival or departure for the King and his visitors at a time when the easiest and safest mode of transport was by barge.

Although the main focus of Henry's building schemes at Hampton Court in the years immediately after his marriage to Anne seems to have been based upon private pleasure and conspicuous display, he did find time to address some practical matters. To the west of the Privy Garden he dug a series of three sunken 'pond yards'. (The excavated earth went to make the conical mound in the Mount Garden.) The rectangular ponds, enclosed within low brick walls, were – like almost everything else in the gardens – surrounded by striped poles bearing carved and painted images of the King's Beasts. Despite this heraldic flourish, the ponds' purpose was strictly functional. They served as storage tanks for live fish destined for the palace kitchens. One pond was used for breeding the fish (mainly carp), while the other two held stock. The basic layout of these ponds can still be seen clearly, although they are now converted into sunken gardens.

Henry's other mundane but necessary innovation at this time was the construction of a giant communal lavatory or 'common jakes' for the lower members of the court. The Great House of Easement, as it was rather euphemistically called, was built out over the moat at the southern end of the West Front. It balanced the service gatehouse at the north end of the façade. Two storeys high, it provided fourteen seats. The sewerage was not directed into the moat itself, but fell straight into the main drain which was regularly flushed with tidal water from the river. The building itself still survives (it is to your right as you approach the main gateway), although it has been converted into office accommodation for the palace.

If Henry showed due concern for the bodily requirements of his court, he did not neglect their spiritual needs. He began a lavish refurbishment of the existing Chapel. A magnificent new fan-vaulted ceiling was installed. Made with oak from the Royal Forest at Windsor, carved by the master craftsmen Richard Ridge and Henry Corrant, it was then painted and gilded in a sumptuous riot of gold and blue (a riot which has since been contributed to by the Victorians, who added a scattering of gold stars). Gilded angels pipe from the giant pendants, and the King's motto – *Dieu et mon Droit* (God and my right) – is picked out in gold letters along the lines of the arches. The richness of the ornament was perhaps achievable because the ceiling had no structural requirements: it was set up under the existing roof beams.

It is all that now remains to remind the visitor of the decorative splendour of Henry's Chapel interior. In his day every surface would have been embellished and patterned. The walls would have been hung with tapestries and paintings, the windows coloured with stained glass, the choir stalls and benches carved and polished, the floor chequered with black and white tiling. Jewel-studded reliquaries and displays of gold plate would have glowed upon the candlelit altars, expressing piety through wealth.

Despite the treasures on view, Henry himself rarely attended the Chapel Royal. He heard Mass in his own closet; the Chapel served the court. It had its own staff, separate from the King's private clergy. Nevertheless, on feast days and other important occasions he would process from the Presence Chamber to the Royal Pew, or Holyday Closet, which looked down on to the Chapel proper. These visits tended to be more a matter of ceremonial display than of devotion. Having arrived in the pew and shown himself to the court, the King would often withdraw to the back of the Holyday Closet and attend to business. If for liturgical reasons he had to descend into the body of the church itself there was a small staircase leading down from the closet.

The Great House of Easement.

Henry, despite leading the English Church to a break with Rome, and despite the advanced Protestant views of his new Queen, was a conservative in liturgical matters. He continued all the old traditional usages: services were said in Latin, relics and religious images adorned the altars, and on Good Friday he maintained the penitential custom of 'creeping to the cross' on his knees (although his courtiers eased his passage for him by laying down cushions as he passed).

FIT FOR A PRINCE

The success of King Henry VIII's ongoing building programme during the mid 1530s could not obscure his growing dissatisfaction with his Queen. Anne was wilful, quick-tempered and prone to jealousy. Scenes were frequent. Hampton Court echoed to her bursts of outrage. Henry refused to engage. If she rebuked him he would simply turn away and leave her. More serious, however, than these domestic spats was Anne's inability to produce a male heir. After the birth of Princess Elizabeth, there was a series of false dawns and disappointments. In 1534 she had a miscarriage. The following year she became pregnant again but the birth was premature. To make matters worse, the stillborn infant was a boy. It is said that this second confinement was precipitated by the Queen's shock at discovering the King amorously embracing one of her ladies-in-waiting. Henry was certainly tiring of Anne.

He had already provoked her wrath with several flirtations before his fancy fell upon the

The richly carved and gilded ceiling of the Chapel Royal.

quiet, solemn, yet not unbeautiful Jane Seymour. He decided that she would make a more satisfactory wife than Anne Boleyn. He looked for an excuse to rid himself of the Queen. Evidence appeared readily to hand to convict her of adultery with two members of the Privy Chamber, a court musician and – for good measure – her own brother. She was sent to the Tower and executed on 19 May 1536. Barely a week later Henry was married to Jane Seymour.

To Henry's way of thinking, a new Queen called for new rooms. His marriage provided a catalyst for a fresh campaign of building and redecoration at Hampton Court.

There was of course the immediate necessity of replacing Anne Boleyn's emblems and initials, so liberally scattered about the palace, with those of the new Queen. The household accounts record a payment for 'xx vanes payntyd an new altered from quene annes armes unto quene janes'. The embossed arms, which can still be seen set on the ceiling of the Great Watching Chamber, are those of the Royal House impaling those of the Seymour family, together with the badges of King Henry and Jane. Nevertheless some of Anne Boleyn's badges and arms were hard to reach. Those on the recently completed roof of the Great Hall had to be left, while the version of her arms set in the vaulting of the gateway between the first two courtyards seems to have been missed by accident.

Henry also effected some changes to the stained glass in the Chapel. He removed the image of his faithless Queen's namesake, St Anne – and also that of St Thomas. This second alteration was perhaps prompted by his exasperation with his intractable and idealistic Chancellor, Thomas More, whom he had had executed the previous year.

The Queen's Lodgings, begun for Anne, were not yet complete, but work continued on them for the benefit of the new Queen. A subtle realignment, however, began to take place. Court protocol was altering. The imposing state chambers were used less and less. Only on very formal occasions would the King appear in the Presence Chamber. The Privy Chamber, however, was becoming ever more crowded. It had become a major forum for discussion and council. The position was recognized and formalized in 1540 with the creation of a designated Privy Council, but it had already existed as a fact for some years. In the face of this pressure upon his space, Henry's response was to increase his own private chambers. He fitted out a new suite of rooms in the gallery on the south side of Cloister Green Court. A similar arrangement was effected in the Queen's Lodgings: her suite of rooms was extended into her gallery on the other side of the courtyard. The scheme marked another step in the royal quest for privacy. In time the east range of Cloister Green Court (originally intended as the Queen's Lodgings) became the private retreat of the King and Queen. They had their private bedrooms and shared reception rooms there.

When Henry and his new wife arrived at Hampton Court in September 1537, the Queen was already heavily pregnant. A special bedchamber was fitted out for her in the most sumptuous, and comfortable, style, with curtains around the bay window and screens around the bed. Henry was clearly confident that Jane would provide him with an heir. He set about converting the gallery that ran between the open and the covered tennis courts into a suite of rooms for the expected child. He also built a new Long Gallery for the Queen, connecting her chambers with the future prince's.

Besides the alteration of the Royal Apartments there was other work to be done. Although the Tudor Court remained peripatetic, its progress had begun to slow. More time was spent at fewer favoured palaces, and Hampton Court was favoured. It had become necessary to improve the water supply. Luckily the means of doing so were at hand. The dissolution of the monasteries, which followed on from Henry's break with Rome, gave the King an opportunity to acquire land in the vicinity of Hampton Court which had previously belonged to Merton Priory. He took possession of the monastic estates at Coombe Hill, three miles from the palace. One freshwater spring rose there, and two others surfaced nearby. Henry set about constructing an elaborate conduit system to pipe this water back to Hampton Court. He spent £50,000 laying lengths of lead pipe. The pipeline ran, underground, via Surbiton, under the Thames (where the pipe was reinforced with an iron casing) and across the palace forecourt.

The water pressure was enough to bring running water up to the King's bathroom on the first floor of the palace. And the constant overflow was used not only to fill the fishponds but also to supply a fountain in the second courtyard.

Henry's optimism was not misplaced. On 12 October, Jane gave birth to the future King Edward VI – the only English monarch to have been born at Hampton Court. Although the child was sickly and the birth had been a difficult one for the mother, Henry was delighted to have a male heir. The whole country rejoiced: bonfires were lit, bells rung and hymns of praise offered up.

The infant prince was christened three days after his birth in the Chapel Royal. The ceremony was rich in both majesty and symbolism. The baby was carried to the chapel in a magnificent procession which wended its way through the State Apartments and the Great Hall, down into the Base Court, through Anne Boleyn's gateway, across the inner court and into the Chapel.

The cortège was led by eighty knights, gentlemen-ushers and squires, walking two-by-two and bearing unlit torches. Behind them came the staff of the Chapel Royal – the choir, the dean and the chaplains. The King's Council followed, and the foreign ambassadors and their retinues. They were followed by two lords bearing a pair of covered basins and 'a cup of assay' for the wine. Next came Anne Boleyn's father, the Earl of Wiltshire, with a towel about his neck, carrying an unlit candle. The Earl of Essex followed him, similarly draped with a towel, and carrying a gold salt 'richly garnished' with pearls and jewels.

Next came the four-year-old Princess Elizabeth carried by two lords, but bearing in her own tiny arms the chrysom oil and a white robe. Behind her was the newborn prince, under a canopy of cloth of gold supported by four gentlemen of the Privy Chamber. He was borne on a cushion by the Marchioness of Exeter, assisted by her husband and by the Duke of Suffolk. The train of the baby's robe was held by the Earl of Arundel, behind whom, in close attendance, were the nurse and midwife. About the royal palanquin walked four more Gentlemen of the Privy Chamber holding torches.

Walking behind the canopy was Princess Mary, Henry's daughter by Catherine of Aragon. She was now twenty-one. Jane Seymour, who had a real affection for her, had persuaded the King to readmit her to the charms of Hampton Court, and she had been assigned a suite of rooms in the Base Court. She was to be the young prince's godmother. After her came 'ladies of honour and gentlewomen in order after their degree'. The route was lined by all the lesser members of the court and household, anxious to catch a first sight of the heir apparent.

The Queen herself, however, was too ill to take part in the procession. She was confined to her Bedchamber, and the King kept her company there.

In the Chapel a special silver font had been set up, raised on a platform, draped and canopied with cloth of gold. Appropriate tapestries had been hung on the walls, and a brazier of hot coals was set nearby to take the autumnal chill off the air.

The christening, however, was soon to be overshadowed by another event. Ten days after the ceremony the Queen died. She was perhaps, it is thought, the victim of the brutal Tudor surgery practised upon her. The King, in his anxiety to secure an heir, had lost a wife. Consumed by grief and, perhaps, remorse, Henry left Hampton Court at once, but the Queen's body remained. It was embalmed, arrayed in gold tissue, and laid out in the Presence Chamber. A crown was set upon her head and jewels upon her hands. Princess Mary and the ladies of the court knelt in vigil about the body while dirges were sung and Masses said. The dead Queen lay in state for a week before being moved to the Chapel, where further prayers were said for her. The body was then taken in solemn procession to Windsor for burial.

The young Prince Edward, however, remained at Hampton Court. He may have been left without a mother but he was soon provided with his own household establishment (under the charge of Sir William Sydney). He had his own suite of rooms at the palace. His lodgings were made on the north-facing range of the Chapel Court. In layout they mimicked those of the King. He had his own Privy Chamber (in reality his nursery) and his own Bedchamber (in which his cradle was attended by its own specially designated 'rockers'). He was

provided, too, with his own bathroom and his own garderobe, which is still visible on the north front of the palace. And he was served by his own Privy Kitchen. Beyond his inward lodgings there was even a Presence Chamber protected by its own Watching Chamber.

King Henry was happy to have secured the line of succession, but other troubles were besetting him. Although only in his forties, he was growing old. The sports of his youth were increasingly beyond his power. He was becoming stout and was subject to bouts of ill-health. In 1536 he suffered a bad fall while hunting and was obliged to all but give up riding for sport.

In 1538 he did lay out a vast Tilt Yard at Hampton Court on the ground to the northwest of the palace but it was never used in earnest

during his lifetime. The little viewing towers, nevertheless, served as very charming and useful banqueting houses. (Although the Tilt Yard was divided up into kitchen-garden plots in the seventeenth century, one of the towers still remains: it is now a tearoom.)

In 1539 Henry enclosed all the lands on the south side of the Thames between Weybridge and Thames Ditton and proclaimed them a royal hunting chase. It was the first new Royal Forest created in almost two centuries. The reason for its creation was set down in the Privy Council minutes some ten years later: 'when hys Highness waxed heavy with sickness, age and corpulency of body, and might not travel so readily abroad, but was constreyned to seke to have hys game and pleasure ready at hand'.

The Family of Henry VIII gives an idea of *Henry VIII's taste in décor.*

But even in these proximous woods the hunting was not what it had been. Unable to ride, Henry hunted from a raised 'standing', shooting with a bow at deer that were flushed from cover and then funnelled past the royal platform between two lines of nets.

Henry's next disappointment was matrimonial. He allowed himself to be persuaded to marry Anne of Cleves. Whatever the diplomatic advantages of the union might have been, they could not outweigh Henry's distaste for the tall, plain, pock-marked girl whom he met, after her disembarkation, at Rochester. 'I like her not,' was his first and enduring impression. Unfortunately

Anne of Cleves's views upon her corpulent, rheumy-eyed fiancé are not recorded. Although the wedding arrangements were too far advanced to be abandoned without an international scandal, the marriage was never consummated. Henry spent the honeymoon arranging for a divorce.

Some of the time that the Queen spent waiting to be released from her matrimonial bonds was passed alone at Hampton Court, but no special preparations seem to have been made for her stay. No scheme of decoration was carried out in her honour. And Henry himself avoided the place.

He returned, however, once the divorce was completed, and brought with him a new betrothed. Catherine Howard had been a lady-in-waiting to Anne of Cleves; she was also a cousin of Anne Boleyn. She was pretty, petite and bewitching, with hazel eyes and lustrous auburn hair. She was also almost thirty years younger than her suitor.

Despite her youth she had already had a number of lovers while under the rather inattentive care of her step-grandmother, the Duchess of Norfolk. At court, moreover, she had fallen in love with a gentleman of the King's Privy Chamber, called Thomas Culpepper. Henry, however, was ignorant of her past liaisons and blind to her present attachments. He showered her with jewels and gifts. He walked with her each evening in the Hampton Court gardens, and sat clasping her hands in shaded arbours and well-appointed window seats. Her head was turned and her vanity flattered by such attentions. Henry married Catherine Howard at Oatlands Palace on 28 July 1540. He presented her at Hampton Court as his new Queen on 8 August 1540.

It was during the first happy days of their marriage here that Henry set up the famous astronomical clock made for him by Nicholas Oursian, Devisor of the King's Horologies. It tells the hour, the month, the day, the number of days since the start of the year, and the phases of the moon; and the time of high water at London Bridge. It was set above the gateway of the inner courtyard, giving the space its enduring name: Clock Court.

Although the clock still stands – and works – time soon ran out for Catherine Howard. She had enemies at court who were only too keen to open the King's eyes to her misdemeanours. On All Souls' Day, 1541, barely eighteen months after her marriage, and only moments after she had heard Mass with the King in the Chapel Royal and had given thanks for their happiness together, her final drama began. During Mass the Archbishop of Canterbury, Thomas Cramner, passed the King a document laying out the full details of Catherine's unfortunate past.

Henry at first refused to believe it. But upon inquiry the stories were confirmed and indeed more came to light. Catherine was confined to her room. At first she denied everything, but eventually with much anguish and lamentation, she confessed. The King would not see her. Legend has it, however, that she managed to escape from her room in the Queen's lodgings and make her way to the Holyday Closet, in the hope of finding the King at Mass. She was caught and escorted, screaming, back along the gallery. She was moved, soon afterwards, to Syon House and from there to the Tower of London. There she was executed on 13 February 1542. Her ghost, however, is still supposed to haunt the gallery outside the Holyday Closet, making its final unavailing plea for mercy.

Catherine's infidelity, and the story of her announcement on the scaffold that, although she died as a Queen, she would rather be dying as the wife of Thomas Culpepper, were blows to King Henry's *amour propre*. His heart was 'pierced with pensiveness' and – uncharacteristically – he gave way to 'plenty of tears'. Nevertheless his spirits rallied and eighteen months later he was persuaded to marry again.

Catherine Parr, his sixth wife, was – at thirty-one – already twice widowed. Her two previous husbands had left her vast estates. Her own family was ambitious; so too was her suitor, Sir Thomas Seymour, brother of Jane Seymour. He was content to surrender her to his sovereign. After the treacherous gaiety of Catherine Howard, Catherine Parr offered the gentle assurance of an even temper and a contented nature. The marriage took place at Hampton Court on 12 July 1543, not in the body of the Chapel but in the Queen's Holyday Closet. The King's two daughters were present.

Hampton Court provided the setting for much of their life together. Henry, in his last burst of building work at the palace, had a new suite of lodgings built for the Queen. They were constructed around the southeast angle of the Base Court.

The palace remained both a haven from care and a showcase for royal magnificence. It was to Hampton Court that Henry invited foreign ambassadors during negotiations as part of the interminable three-cornered dispute between France, the Holy Roman Empire and England. At the end of 1541 he had entertained the Emperor's envoy, Ferdinando de Gonzaga, 'Viceroy of Sicily, Prince of Malfeta and Captain-General of the Army of the Emperor Charles', together with his retinue. Plans were laid for an invasion of France the following year.

The allies' campaign proved successful. The next important state reception at Hampton Court, in August 1546, was for the French ambassador, Claude d'Annebant, Lord High Admiral of France, who came to ratify a treaty ending the war. It was the last, and perhaps the greatest, of the receptions held at the palace. To accommodate the 200 gentlemen of the French retinue, an encampment of gold and velvet tents was erected in the grounds around the palace.

Henry exerted himself to impress. But he found his duties onerous. His health had suffered another serious decline: he was tormented – amongst other ailments – by an ulcerated leg. Although only fifty-three, he had become old and immobile. Increasingly he sought to introduce his young heir to the duties of royal power. The eight-year-old Prince Edward was sent out at the head of a troop of 540 liveried men, to greet the ambassador and his entourage. He escorted the party back to the palace, where it was welcomed by the Lord Chancellor and members of the King's Council.

Only on the following morning did the ambassador finally meet the King himself. Henry received Admiral d'Annebant in the Presence Chamber. He then accompanied him to hear Mass in the Chapel Royal. Before breaking the host the ambassador swore to honour the new treaty. The service was followed by a week of banqueting, masques and entertainments as lavish as anything Henry had ever produced.

Henry's personal diversions, however, were becoming increasingly sedentary. He could still manage the occasional game of bowls, but backgammon and cards were easier for an obese man with a gammy leg. And he continued to find pleasure and consolation in music. His building work at Hampton Court had come to a halt. Although he spent the end of 1546 at the palace, he returned to London early in the new year, and it was there that he died on 28 January 1547.

THE MUSIC FESTIVAL

*H*ampton Court has always been a place of festivity and show. It was designed to impress. The palace was fitted out as an ideal setting for revels, routs and entertainment. Both Wolsey and Henry VIII used it as the scene for lavish displays of hospitality. And these glorious occasions have found an echo down the ages, from the masques of James I's time to the theatrical performances of the early Georgian period. In 1964 the Great Hall was used for a production of *Twelfth Night*, and four years later it was the setting for a gala ballet performance in honour of the President of Turkey. In recent years, however, the palace has returned to something like its former festive glory.

Each summer the palace plays host to a music festival. It runs for a week in the middle of June and attracts many of the world's great musical performers, from Montserrat Caballé and José Carreras to Nigel Kennedy and Vanessa Mae. The highlights in 1998 included performances by Lesley Garrett and Paco Pena. The festival ends with a glorious firework display over the gardens. Rather than using the Great Hall, a temporary, open-air auditorium is established in the Base Court.

The festival is a massive logistical operation, quite on a par with the great events staged at the Tudor Court to impress visiting dignitaries. The independent organizers marshal a team of fifty

A juggler entertaining the crowds.

people to build a complete orchestral stage and a grandstand with 2,700 seats. They lay over twelve miles of cable and rig up more than 1,200 lights. And all this is accomplished inside a week.

The performance nights themselves require military planning. Teams of ushers are needed to marshal people into their seats. Although a train service runs – by special arrangement – from Hampton Court station to London fifteen minutes after the end of each performance, many of the concert patrons arrive by chauffeur-driven car; it can be a recipe for traffic jams, delays and the more genteel sort of road rage.

Open-air entertainment also presents inevitable problems with the weather. The British summer can usually be relied upon for a good dose of rain. 'That's when the true British bulldog spirit comes into it,' says Dennis McGuinnes. 'They'll sit there with their brollies and disposable macs. But,' he admits, 'the performers are another matter. The musicians, quite rightly, are very concerned about their instruments. They'll be the first to disappear.'

The Tudor notion of having music as a background to dining has not been adopted exactly, but during each performance there is a seventy-five minute interval when the concert-goers can picnic in the gardens or eat in grand style in the State Apartments. The atmosphere of cultural diversion and expansive leisure would have appealed to many of the monarchs who resided at Hampton Court – but perhaps most to Henry VIII.

Festival goers are encouraged to picnic in the palace gardens.

Henry was certainly the most musical king in English history. He not only loved listening to music, he played it and even composed it. Musicians, minstrels and choristers were in almost constant attendance upon him and he greatly increased the number of performers at court. He gathered the finest talents from across Europe (very much as the festival organizers do) and established a special group of singers and instrumentalists called The King's Musick, which was dedicated to his service.

He also took an active role in their performances. He had a fine voice and was able to accompany himself on the organ, harpsichord or lute. During the summer of 1510 it is recorded that he amused himself with playing the recorder, flute and virginals, as well as with the 'setting of songs' and 'making of ballads'. It is also noted that he 'did set two goodly masses, every of them five parts'. Two of Henry's motets, 'O Lord, the Maker of all things' and 'Quam pulchra es', are still in the repertoire.

His secular music has been no less enduring. His setting of 'Greensleeves' is a perennial favourite, while his most famous lyric, 'Pastance with good company' , begins with the telling declaration:

Pastance with good company
I love and shall until I die
Grudge who will, but none deny,
So God be pleased this life will I
For my pastance,
Hunt, sing, and dance,
My heart is set,
All goodly sport
To my comfort
Who shall me let?

The lines could almost serve as the *raison d'être* for the current festivals programme at Hampton Court.

Henry, however, as master of his own house, was able to arrange matters to please himself. The current festival organizers are constrained by a host of special considerations. The historic fabric of the palace has to be protected and maintained. This presents problems for the caterers who arrange the dinners inside the palace buildings. All the floral displays for the tables have to be made outside and then carried into place, to prevent the possibility of water or pollen damage. Candles have to be kept low, to prevent heat or smoke damaging the ceilings. Red wine is not allowed. (Dennis McGuinnes still speaks ruefully about the 'red wine stain on the King's Stairs' that dates from his first year at the palace.) All the food, linen and cutlery has to be prepared, set out and cleared away within the day – and all under the anxious eyes of the palace housekeeping team.

One particular area of anxiety is sticky tape: it is, apparently, a vital component in any catering operation, used for holding paper tablecloths in place or sticking up instructions for staff. Yet even masking tape can cause severe damage to old surfaces. The housekeeping team, however, have discovered a special 'low-tack tape' which can be applied safely. They insist that all private contractors use it. It is the sort of attention to detail that would have impressed a Tudor despot.

The music festival ends in spectacular fashion with a firework display.

FLORAL FASHIONS

Hampton Court did not stop developing after it was given over to the public by Queen Victoria. In some areas there was a concerted attempt to return things to their original form. Many architectural elements of the palace structure were carefully restored to their original Tudor design. The gardens and grounds, however, were allowed to take on a more contemporary aspect.

For the Victorians, a 'contemporary aspect' meant blazing displays of bedding plants arranged in formal patterns in rectangular flowerbeds. It was a look that was achieved with great effect on the eastern lawns of the palace gardens. The 'profusion of blossom and the gorgeousness of colour' during the summer months was spectacular, according to contemporary accounts.

The effect was rather too eye-catching for some. Ernest Law, the guardian of the palace's history – and designer of the Knot Garden – was not impressed. He considered the new look most inappropriate. He lamented what he called the 'attempts to follow the fluctuating follies of successive fashions in gardening… by efforts to vie with the costly pretentiousness of the modern style'. He was very relieved that when they came to plant the great herbaceous border running along the Broadwalk they adopted a more naturalistic approach.

Graham Dillamore (right) and Gary Wise discuss the finer points of topiary.

Time, however, plays strange tricks. The High Victorian phase of the gardens has now become part of Hampton Court's history. And it is a part that is preserved and celebrated in some of the gardening work carried out now.

Graham Dillamore, the Deputy Gardener at the palace, has a genuine affection for the style. 'Hampton Court has got this great tradition of Victorian bedding,' he enthuses. 'It was Hampton Court which really originated this style of plant use in the summer season. And the whole personality of the garden on the East Front is still very Victorian, so we try and follow their traditional methods and colour schemes. We also try to use as many Victorian plants as possible. The heliotrope and the canna, for example, were great Victorian favourites and they give a real feel of the era.'

Nevertheless, as with other areas of the gardens, the desire for historical authenticity is tempered by both practical and aesthetic considerations. Budgets are not what they were in the late nineteenth century. 'We need flowers that are going to last all the summer,' explains Graham somewhat ruefully. 'If a plant's going to flower in June and then fizzle out, that's no good. It has got to last from the first week of June, when we put it in, right the way through to the end of September.'

And although the style is founded upon the Victorian model there is still scope for innovation and self-expression. Bedding out, as Graham recognizes, has rather an unfair image: 'Most people envisage plants in straight lines, with everything standing to attention. That doesn't have to be the case,' he points out. 'A flowerbed may be square, but the actual bedding design within it doesn't have to be square at all; you can have circles, curves, triangles.' He has tried to introduce these ideas into his own work. 'I used to follow the line of the beds, squaring each border off and planting in blocks,' he admits. 'But I have since started to use more curves, to break up the rigidity of the design.'

Henry VIII's old Pond Garden (which was subsequently Queen Mary's 'flower garden') has become one of the principal settings for the bedding-out displays. 'It's a great canvas to work on,' says Graham, 'because it can only be viewed from one place – from the outside looking in. That gives the designer an awful lot of scope to play around with different patterns and effects.'

Certainly it is one of the most arresting places in the grounds. The beds, stepped at different levels, are a riot of colour and texture during the summer months: begonias, heliotrope, stocks, zinnias, geraniums, African marigolds, ageratum and other less easily recognized specimens jostle in profusion.

And at the centre of this festival of colour stands a lead statue of Venus, brought from Windsor at some point in the nineteenth century as a not entirely adequate exchange for the four statues removed from the parapet of the South Front. The display draws gasps from the procession of visitors who pause at the gate to look in.

'The Pond Garden,' says Graham, 'has always been a place where the gardener can be bit creative, where he can demonstrate his art if you like. You are governed by some historical integrity but on the whole you can use that garden to demonstrate a whole range of colour schemes. In the beds on the East Front you are much more closely governed by the traditional Victorian theme, but here I can let my imagination run riot, and really experiment with colours – try out a few different things.'

Graham says he is constantly learning and experimenting. 'The inspiration for this year's Pond Garden scheme really grew out of last year's. I felt that last year the colours were far too scattered across the beds. This time I've tried to broaden the beds out and to use the colours for a longer time and more strongly.' The dominating theme is mauve, offset by notes of yellow, pink and red. 'I've tried to bring a strong mauve right the way through the garden,' explains Graham, 'starting with the top layer of beds. They're the most important, because they're the biggest, and they're the first thing that most people see. The effect has got to be "Bang! Zap!" I certainly don't want people walking past.'

Colour is vital to the success of bedding-out schemes and it has to be used with confidence. Graham has learnt from his mistakes. 'I used white in the Pond Garden once,' he confesses. 'I thought it would be quite good – light and airy. I used it with a little bit of pink, which is usually quite successful. But it just disappeared completely. It got completely lost. There's too much white in the sky to use it as a major colour in a planting scheme. It looked awful.'

For Graham the Victorians remain the masters of the art. 'They really knew how to use bedding,' he explains. 'They would be quite bold and extravagant with their use of colour – reds, yellows, oranges, pinks, mauves, purples – and quite rightly so. Hampton Court was a royal palace and they wanted to make a statement. I'd back them all the way,' he adds. 'Thank God for the Victorians.'

The Pond Garden in its glory.

GHOSTS

'One of the first things we get asked,' says Ian Franklin, 'is where are the ghosts?' Ian is a warder at Hampton Court and, in an effort to answer this question as fully as possible, he has devoted much of his free time to compiling a dossier of all the apparently supernatural phenomena experienced by staff and visitors to the palace. In a little over a year he has gathered an impressive body of first-hand testimony.

'I am a sceptic myself,' he admits. 'But I think that's good. It introduces an element of "quality control", if you like.' Nevertheless he has been forced to recognize that people – many people – do experience 'strange things'. He has learnt of numerous incidents, spectral sightings, powerful but unexplained sensations, things that go bump in the night. The palace, it seems, has a far more active spirit life than has generally been supposed.

Traditionally only three ghosts were ascribed to Hampton Court: two Queens and a royal nurse. And Catherine Howard, King Henry VIII's unfortunate fifth wife, seems to be the most restless of the trio. Her anguished cries and pounding footsteps are said to echo down the corridor along which she ran in her attempt to reach the King in the Royal Pew and plead for mercy. Some people are even said to have seen her form reach the door of the pew and then turn back 'with disordered garments and a ghastly look of despair'. The

Ian Franklin in the 'Haunted Gallery'.

corridor, as a result, has come to be known as the 'Haunted Gallery'. It is one of the most visited parts of the palace. 'It's very popular with the Japanese,' says Ian. 'I think it was featured in a Japanese documentary about Hampton Court.' There is an irony in this because, as Ian notes, the gallery is certainly not the most haunted place in the palace. Catherine's ghost has not been sighted for many years. Even in the late nineteenth century, when Ernest Law wrote his history of Hampton Court, he could only find evidence of people who had heard – but not seen – the spirit. Two grace-and-favour residents, Lady Eastlake and Mrs Cavendish Boyle, did both assert – independently – that they had heard piercing and 'unearthly' shrieks coming from the gallery during the 'dead of night'. One historian of the palace has suggested that the whole legend of the Haunted Gallery was made up by residents who wanted to get better apartments.

Jane Seymour's spectre is accounted to be altogether quieter, as she herself was in life. There have been sightings of her ghost, just around the corner from the Haunted Gallery, on the stairs and in the adjacent Silver Stick Gallery. She has appeared as a pallid form, clothed in white and carrying a lighted taper. The reason for her regret is unclear. Perhaps, it has been suggested, she is consumed by remorse at having usurped the place of her mistress, Anne Boleyn, in the affections of the King and thus contributed to her death.

Dennis McGuinnes has tales to tell.

The palace's third famous ghost is less exalted. After Queen Jane Seymour died, her sickly son was nursed by a woman called Sibell Penn. Mistress Penn seems to have been the sister-in-law of Sir William Sydney, who was in charge of the infant Prince's household arrangements. She became a trusted and esteemed royal servant. When her charge became King Edward VI she was granted rooms at Hampton Court. It was there, in 1562, that she contracted smallpox and died. She was buried in Hampton Church and a life-sized marble effigy of her was set above the grave.

In 1829 the church was demolished and, although the effigy and tomb were preserved and moved to the Chapel Royal, the grave itself was, 'irreverently disturbed and her remains scattered'. Another account, however, claims that all that was found when the grave was opened was a hairpin and a lock of hair.

Certainly, soon after the desecration odd things began to be reported at the palace. A strange, low, rhythmical noise was heard, apparently coming from behind a wall in the southwest wing of the palace. After this inexplicable phenomenon had been noted by several people, action was decided upon. The wall was broken down and a small, and unknown, room was discovered. It contained an old spinning wheel, and it was noticed that the oak floorboards were worn away where the treadle struck the floor.

It was suggested that Sibell Penn, after being disturbed in her grave, had returned to the room she had worked in – and the wheel she had worked – during her life. Although her spinning wheel has been removed, her ghostly form, clad in a long, grey hooded robe, is still abroad. Towards the end of the last century a guard was terrified to see her tall, gaunt figure, her arms outstretched before her, walk by him and then pass through a wall. And Princess Frederica of Hanover is supposed to have discovered the ghost in the nursery of her ill-fated baby. Mistress Penn has not, however, been seen back at her former workroom.

Besides this distinguished trio, Ernest Law records one other supernatural presence. In 1871, while workmen were laying a new drainage system under Wren's arcade in Fountain Court, two skeletons were discovered. There was much debate as to who they might have been. Popular sentiment suggested that one was Lord Francis Villiers, the dashing younger brother of the Duke of Buckingham, who was killed in a skirmish near Kingston at the start of the Second Civil War. But the identification is implausible, not least because Lord Francis's body is in fact buried in Westminster Abbey. Nevertheless, the skeletons probably dated from the seventeenth century and their hasty and unmarked interment does suggest that their end might well have been connected with some unrecorded event of the war.

After the discovery the remains were properly buried, to the great relief of one of the elderly grace-and-favour residents of the palace. As she remarked at the time, 'The stupid Board of Works has at last found the two wretched men who, I have been telling everyone, have been haunting me for years.' She had been constantly disturbed by rapping sounds, and by the uneasy sense that two unseen beings were close at hand. The two unquiet souls now seem to have achieved peace; they have stopped pestering the residents.

Ian's research has charted the way some of these legends have grown over the years, and has also added greatly to the list of visiting spirits. Nor are all these ghosts in human form. He has heard tales of a spectral cat that haunts the threshold of the tour office in Clock Court, and of a ghostly dog than has been heard on the King's Stairs.

Despite Ian's healthy attitude of doubt, he admits that on occasion 'scepticism gets strained right to the limit'. When, for instance, three different and unconnected sources all recount sightings of the same 'monk-like cowled figure' under similar circumstances, he is inclined to believe that *something* must lie behind it.

The force of some testimony is also too compelling to ignore. Dennis McGuinnes – who describes himself as not so much a sceptic as a cynic – has told Ian of some very curious incidents that he has witnessed. Initially Dennis and his wife Sylvia lived in Apartment 15 in Fountain Court. They were aware that the previous tenant had reported 'poltergeist' type happenings. In her sitting room the pictures were regularly flung off the walls during the night. In the end she changed

the room into her dining room so that she did not have to go into it so often. The McGuinneses returned it to its original use, but soon became aware of a strange aura about the place.

Dennis recalls being alone in the apartment one evening. 'I passed the half-open doorway of the sitting room. I believed I saw a shape in there. I paused. And then went back and looked in. I could see nothing there of course. But then I felt the hair on my arms stand on end, then the hairs on the back of my neck. And as I went on up the stairs I felt as though two padded planks were pressing against the sides of my head.'

These vague sensations, however, became much more defined when the McGuinneses moved into a new set of rooms. Some members of the family soon began to be aware of a strange presence. In the sitting room Dennis would become 'aware of someone coming into the doorway'. He would look up and see a female figure: 'It was always the same figure, very short, in a blue – dark blue – cloak. The material of the cloak was heavy, like velvet. And it was always in the same place: in the doorway.' At a second look the figure always disappears, sometimes retreating down the corridor beyond the doorway, sometimes passing out of sight, as though into the wall. So vivid is the apparition that on one occasion Dennis followed after it, calling, 'Please come back and speak to me.'

Dennis himself remains bemused by these inexplicable experiences, and wary of them. However, his wife contacted a transmedium about the phenomenon and was told that the figure was probably the ghost of someone called Olwyn, who was a lady-in-waiting to Catherine of Aragon. As the McGuinneses' sitting room was Queen Catherine's Presence Chamber there is an intriguing plausibility about the suggestion…

CHAPTER 3

THE SEAT OF PLEASURE

Henry's three children had all spent part of their childhoods at Hampton Court, and they spent time there too in the coming years as each in turn received the crown. Many dramatic incidents of late-sixteenth-century royal history were played out within the palace walls. Yet the walls themselves actually changed little. Henry's enthusiasm for building projects was not matched by his heirs. It did not need to be. His vision and energy had left his children with many magnificent palaces. They were content to maintain and enjoy them. Hampton Court was amongst the most magnificent and the most readily enjoyed.

Edward VI came to the palace soon after acceding to the throne. He was only nine. A delicate, studious child, he found the quiet and calm of Hampton Court beneficial to his health and to his studies. His affection for what he called

OPPOSITE Edward VI, the only English monarch to be born at Hampton Court. ABOVE Another of the King's Beasts.

'Ampton Court' is revealed in many of his diary entries. During his minority power was invested, according to Henry's deathbed instructions, in a Council of Regency. But the Council was dominated by Edward Seymour, one of Jane Seymour's brothers, and he soon assumed a preeminent position as Lord Protector. He was given the title of Duke of Somerset. With Edward cloistered at Hampton Court, he exercised power almost at his own discretion.

Somerset's policies soon proved disastrous. He embarked on an ill-fated war against the Scots, which served only to provoke their old allies, the French, into entering the fray on their side. His campaigns placed a fresh strain on an already weakened economy. He was obliged to debase the coinage. Popular rebellions broke out against his rule. The Council of Regency moved to strip him of his position. Somerset, however, tried to outmanoeuvre them. He held, he thought, the trump card.

A seventeenth century panorama of Hampton Court,
viewed from the east.

He was at Hampton Court with the young King. He sought to present the Council's move as an act of treachery against the sovereign, rather than as an act of restraint against himself. He issued proclamations to this effect, and urged all loyal subjects of the Crown to rally to the King.

The appeal was, at first, successful. Men from the local towns and villages converged outside Hampton Court, armed and ready to defend their King. In London, however, the Council members were able to explain the true position more clearly: their animus was against Somerset, not King Edward. Further support for the Protector failed to materialize. In desperation Somerset tried to barricade himself and the King into the palace. He ranged cannons about the walls and he refilled the moat. But it soon became clear to him that Hampton Court had been built for pleasure not defence. Its perimeter was too vast to man, its structure – of brick and glass – too weak to sustain an assault. He made an impassioned appeal to the crowds at the gate, asking for their continued support. But he could sense that their mood was

turning against him. Fearing attack from London, Somerset decided that he must abandon the palace. He gathered up the King, who was suffering from a heavy cold, and – under cover of darkness – rode with him to Windsor, where the castle offered greater hope of protection.

The move, however, only delayed the inevitable. Somerset, after bargaining for his own life, was obliged to surrender his power. He was sent to the Tower. King Edward returned, once more, to the gardens and galleries of Hampton Court and tried to recapture there the sense of calm which had been so recently and so violently disturbed.

The prime mover in the coup against Somerset was the Earl of Warwick. He soon began to assume many of the Protector's powers. He, like his King, belonged to the Protestant party within the English Church, and when the Council convened at Hampton Court in July 1551 it was his influence that persuaded the councillors to issue the famous

Proclamation to the English bishops, urging them to 'resort more diligently' to the recently authorized *Book of Common Prayer* which offered services in English rather than Latin.

The magnificence of the palace remained undimmed. It was still regarded as a wonder to be seen. The Queen Dowager of Scotland, Mary of Guise, made a special detour to admire the house. And Edward continued to use the place to impress visiting dignitaries. In July 1551 he received the French envoy, Maréchal de St André, together with his retinue. The finest tapestries were put on display. After a formal audience with the King, and a Mass in the Chapel Royal, a feast was prepared in the Great Hall. The evening, we are told, was passed 'with great revelry'. As a mark of especial favour the Maréchal was invited to attend an 'arraying', a reception held, not in the Privy Chamber but in the more intimate confines of the State Bedchamber. This was a recent innovation, marking a new stage in court ceremonial.

If the splendour of the palace was maintained, the extent of the grounds was not. The simmering local resentment at Henry VIII's transformation of the great swathe of common land between Weybridge and Thames Ditton into a Royal Chase broke out with the old King's death. The Council was petitioned, and it was agreed that the deer and the palings should be removed. The land itself, though, was never officially 'dechased', in case the new King should ever wish to lay claim to it. It still exists nominally as a Royal Chase.

The last dramatic event to disturb the calm of Hampton Court during the short reign of Edward VI was the arrest of the Duke of Somerset. By 1551 Somerset had manoeuvred himself back into a position of influence within the Regency Council, and he was conspiring to resume full control.

Warwick, however, outflanked him. The Council was meeting at Hampton Court due to an epidemic of the 'sweating sickness' that was then raging in London. Somerset, however, was barred from attending because one of his servants had contracted the disease. His absence allowed Warwick to marshal his own support and persuade the King of the threat that Somerset posed. After a brief period of quarantine Somerset was summoned to attend the Council. He was arrested in the Council Chamber at the palace and charged with conspiracy against the Council.

He was subsequently taken to the Tower for trial, and executed at the beginning of 1552. Edward VI survived him by only eighteen months: he died at Greenwich on 6 July 1553, aged fifteen.

Mary I after Sir Anthony van Dyck.

In the aftermath of the King's death, Warwick made an ill-fated attempt to place the crown on the head of his daughter-in-law, Lady Jane Grey. But he was thwarted. Henry VIII's elder daughter, Mary, ascended to the throne. Although recognized as the rightful heir, she was regarded with some suspicion: she was a Catholic and she was a woman. England had never been ruled by a woman before. Mary, moreover, was unmarried and almost forty.

It was thought prudent that she should marry. She was anxious to produce an heir. Ignoring the advice of her councillors she sought an alliance with Philip II of Spain, the son of the Holy Roman Emperor. As a Spaniard – and fellow Catholic – he was not a popular choice with Mary's new subjects.

They were married first by proxy, and then again when Philip arrived in England in July 1554. They spent their honeymoon together at Hampton Court. It was a muted affair. The palace, once the scene of feasting and revelry, became quiet and sober. Philip's reserved, proud and surreptitious manner did little to dissolve the prejudice of the English courtiers.

By the end of the year, noting the swelling of her stomach, Mary became convinced that she was pregnant. In the spring of 1555 she returned with her consort to Hampton Court in order that the child might be born there. She retreated from public life in preparation for the event. A royal nursery was made ready and decorated. Midwives and nurses were all engaged. A cradle, 'veri sumptuouslie and gorgouslie trimmed', was built, we are told, and carved with the ditty:

The child which Thou to Marie
O Lord of might hast send,
To England's joie in health
Preserve, keepe and defend.

Sadly it is no longer amongst the treasures of Hampton Court. Masses of expectation and thanksgiving were said. Special documents were prepared announcing the birth of the royal child, leaving only a blank space for the child's sex to be added. Messengers stood by, ready to carry these notices to the far corners of Europe. Their wait was a long one.

On 23 April, St George's Day, after a high Mass in the Chapel Royal, Philip led a solemn procession of lords and clerics around the palace courts and cloisters. Mary, to dispel the rumour that she had died, appeared at her window as the procession passed by.

Although her appearance did something to scotch immediate rumours, there remained a real fear that she *would* die in childbirth. It was a prospect viewed with some alarm. Philip was officially co-sovereign with his Queen; if Mary should die but her child survive, he would be poised to rule as regent. He was, however, specifically excluded from rule should Mary die without child. In that case the succession would pass either to Mary's sister Elizabeth, or to their cousin, Mary Queen of Scots. Elizabeth, it seems, was the preferred of the two, although as a Protestant she was deeply suspect in her sister's eyes. Elizabeth was summoned to Hampton Court to be present at the birth. She was not, however, welcomed as a royal sister. She was placed under house arrest.

At the beginning of the year Sir Thomas Wyatt had led a rebellion, not against the Queen's person, but against her policies, and particularly her religious policies. Mary suspected that Elizabeth might be implicated in the insurrection. Mary installed her sister not in the palace proper but in the Water Gallery at the far end of the Privy

Garden. From there Elizabeth followed what she could of the unfolding drama.

The day expected for the birth of Mary's child arrived. The Queen went into what she insisted was labour. But the day passed and no child arrived. Doctors were duly summoned. Fresh examinations were made. It was discovered that there was no child. The Queen was not pregnant at all. Her distended stomach was merely the result of dropsy.

Philip began to realize that his chances of producing an heir to the English throne were now very scant indeed. Mary felt crushed by the disappointment and by her inability to provide her husband with what he wanted. The matter of the succession came more sharply into focus. Elizabeth, confined to the Water Gallery, received a succession of deputations from Mary's Privy Councillors, and indeed from Philip himself, all urging her to seek the Queen's forgiveness and clemency for whatever part she might have played in the Wyatt Rebellion. Elizabeth, sure of her own innocence, stoutly claimed that she would not ask forgiveness for something that she was not guilty of. She professed complete loyalty to her sister, and – though she knew herself to be undeserving of it – she refused to complain of the treatment that she was receiving at her hands.

Unable to elicit any hint of complicity, Queen Mary finally summoned her sister before her in the State Bedchamber. The scene was calculated to impress: Mary seated by torchlight on a chair of estate and Elizabeth kneeling before her. But Elizabeth was unawed. She continued to maintain her innocence with unwavering meekness. In exasperation Mary finally rose from her chair, exclaiming '*Sabe Dios*' (God knows), and left the room.

Elizabeth was escorted back to her rooms in the Water Gallery. But a week later her freedom was returned to her.

Mary left the palace soon afterwards. Her subsequent visits were rare, those of her husband rarer. She did go there with Philip in the summer of 1557 'to hunt and kill a great hart with certain of the Council'. And she returned a final time in August of the following year. She had convinced herself again that she was expecting a child. In fact her health was collapsing. After a fruitless wait for the non-existent heir she moved on again. She died that November.

LEISURE AND RETREAT

Queen Elizabeth, during her long reign, used Hampton Court mainly as a place of private leisure and retreat. Her Council did meet at the palace during the winter of 1568 to decide the fate of Mary Queen of Scots, but such intrusions of state business were rare.

When in residence Elizabeth preferred to wander in the gardens, hunt in the park and entertain her favoured courtiers in the galleries and chambers. Unlike her two siblings, Elizabeth even effected some minor improvements to the palace. Her alterations were small but telling. She installed a bay window in the south range, looking out on to what is now – and was also perhaps then – a little Knot Garden. The two plaques, carved with her initials and the date (1568), which were set into the stonework of the new window, can still be seen. To banish noxious smells she moved her Privy Kitchen from its place under her private apartments to a more distant position at the easternmost end of the kitchen range. It is still in use, as has been mentioned, as the 'Privy Kitchen Coffee Shop'. She extended the stable block on Hampton Court Green, just outside the gates, to house the coaches that had recently been acquired as the most modern and convenient form of land conveyance. Previously she – like her forebears – had been obliged either to ride or to travel on a lumbering unsprung wagon. The stables still stand, their date of construction inscribed on their lead drainpipe heads.

She also replaced the heraldic fountain that Henry VIII had set up in Clock Court with a more magnificent and up-to-date structure. In the centre of the basin was a statue of Justice supported on columns of black and white marble. It was a source of both wonder and diversion. The Duke of Württemberg, on a visit to the palace in 1592, described it as a 'splendid, high and massy fountain, with a waterwork, by which you can, if you like, make the water play upon the ladies and others who are standing by, and give them a thorough wetting'. Sadly this amusing device (along with the rest of the fountain) has been dismantled and lost.

Beyond these structural additions and alterations, Elizabeth devoted money and time to enriching the already lavish decor of the palace. She added, too, to the palace's unrivalled collection of tapestries, commissioning a whole series depicting her naval victories against the Spanish. Even the French ambassador was impressed by the effect she created. 'I have seen,' he recorded, 'in the palaces of Windsor and Hampton Court, but especially at the latter, more riches and costly furniture than I ever did see, or could have imagined.' In the room called Paradise she placed a spectacular curiosity, a musical instrument made entirely out of glass.

Nor did the garden and park escape the Queen's attention. During the winter months it was her habit to rise early and take a brisk walk in the gardens, in order to 'catch her a hete in the colde mornings'. On less private occasions, it seems, she would proceed at a rather more sedate pace; as one courtier noted, 'she, who was the very image of majesty and magnificence, went slowly and marched with leisure, and with a certain grandity rather than gravity'. To amuse herself on these progresses through the garden and grounds she created 'sundry towers, or rather bowers, for places of recreation and solace, and for sundry other uses'. These pleasure spots were decked with rosemary, roses and other sweet-scented flowers which were 'trained, intertwined and trimmed in so wonderful a manner, and in such extraordinary shapes, that the like could not easily be found'.

The secluded arbours lent a romantic atmosphere to the place, and Elizabeth was delighted to enhance the effect by every means possible. Even her hunting expeditions were dressed in the language of poetry. When out in the park she might repair to 'a delicate bower, under which were her Highness' musicians placed, and a cross-bow by a nymph, with a sweet song, delivered to her hands to shoot at the deer'.

The palpable aura of romance that surrounded Hampton Court, although it amused the Queen and impressed her courtiers, also gave rise to gossip. Hostile rumour suggested that Elizabeth used the palace as a place of assignation with her favourite, Lord Robert Dudley (the future Earl of Leicester). There was even a suggestion that in the spring of 1561 the Queen had actually given birth to Dudley's child within the sheltered seclusion of Hampton Court.

A contemporary painting of Queen Elizabeth I. 'Good Queen Bess' used Hampton Court principally as a place of private retreat.

The Royal Mews as they are today.

The rumour had a long currency. Over twenty years later a young man called Arthur Sotheran even presented himself at the Spanish court claiming to be that illegitimate child. The man who had raised him and given him his name, he explained, had been summoned clandestinely to Hampton Court one night. There he had been met by Nicholas Haryngton, one of the Queen's officers, who explained to him 'that a lady at Court had been delivered of a child, [and] that the Queen was desirous to conceal her dishonour'. Sotheran was then 'led into the gallery near the royal closet' where he was given the baby, and instructed to call it Arthur. He took the child to his home, reared him, sent him to school and then completed his education abroad. Arthur claimed that he only learnt of his 'true parentage' at his supposed-father's deathbed. Arthur Sotheran's claims to royal blood can almost certainly be discounted, but they suggest something of the whiff of scandal that

hovered around Hampton Court during the reign of 'Good Queen Bess'.

Elizabeth and her court celebrated Christmas at the palace on several occasions. These were periods of great feasting and revelling. The days were passed in sports and games, the nights in eating, dancing and other entertainments. On almost every night between Christmas Eve and Twelfth Night a masque or play was performed in the Great Hall. The 'Accounts of the revels at Court' give some idea of the splendour of these productions. Money was paid out to an army of carpenters, carvers and joiners to erect a stage at the west end of the Hall under the Minstrels' Gallery. Scenery was made. One production called for 'houses made of canvas, framed and painted accordingly as might serve their several purposes'; another necessitated the painting of 'seven cities, one village, and one country house'. Trees were brought in to create the illusion of a forest.

Lighting for these productions was provided by tiny oil lamps hung from wires stretched across the breadth of the Hall. The actors changed in the pantry outside the west end of the Hall. The plays performed over Christmas 1576 included *The Painter's Daughter*, 'enacted by the Earl of Warwick's servants', *Toolie* by Lord Howard's servants, *The History of the Collyer*, 'enacted by the Earl of Leicester's men' and *The History of Error* (perhaps the inspiration for Shakespeare's *Comedy of Errors*) 'enacted by the Children of Pawles'.

New Year, rather than Christmas, was the time for present-giving. A record is preserved of all the 'New Year's Gifts' presented and received by the Queen at Hampton Court at the beginning of 1578. The whole court was expected to give something, and although the Queen would repay the compliment, she invariably got the better of the exchange. Her gifts tended to be token items of silver-gilt, while those that she received were more varied and more valuable. That year the Countess of Derby gave her 'a petticoat of white satin raised and edged with a broad embroidery of divers colours'. The Earl of Leicester produced a spectacular 'carcanet of gold, enamelled, garnished with sparks of diamonds and rubies and pendants of pearls', while Lord Burleigh adopted the most expedient course, and gave cash: he presented Her Majesty with £30.

The connection in the Queen's mind between Hampton Court and pleasure seems to have persisted to the end. The last visit she paid to the palace was in the summer of 1599. She came with only a small retinue and stayed only a few days. There were no organized festivities. But a courtier, looking in through a casement, saw her 'dancing the Spanish Panic to a whistle and taboureur, none being with her but my Lady Warwick'. The Queen died four years later, on 24 March 1603, aged sixty-nine.

MASQUES AND PHASES

James VI of Scotland's accession to the English throne as James I marked no falling away in the popularity of Hampton Court. The new King was passionate about hunting and the park at Hampton Court provided very convenient sport. The King's actual aptitude for the chase may be doubted. Bandy-legged, weak-kneed, goggle-eyed and 'naturally of a timorous disposition', he was not a born huntsman. Nevertheless he had convinced himself that stag-hunting represented an important part of his royal duty and he exerted himself to fulfil it. Often he would ignore the pressing

King James I by Paul van Somer.

Anne of Denmark by Paul van Somer.

business of state in order to go hunting. And even when he did attend to government he could not be relied upon to forget his favourite topic. He issued a stinging 'Proclamation against Hunters, Stealers and Killers of deare' from Hampton Court, in September 1609, claiming that they were spoiling his sport. And he followed it up with an attack on the 'old and barbarous insolence of multitudes of vulgar people, who, pressing upon us in our sports as we are hunting, do ride over our dogs, brake their backs, spoil our game, run over and destroy the corn, and not without great annoyance and sometimes peril both to our own person and to our dearest son the prince, by their heedless riding and galoping'.

The King hunted either on horseback with hounds or from a standing with a longbow. On the latter occasions he would attend the meet resplendent in an outfit 'green as the grass he trod on, with a feather in his cap, and a horne instead of a sword by his side'. Many of his courtiers considered the effect more ridiculous than dashing.

Given the King's enthusiasm, it is not surprising to learn that such work as he carried out at Hampton Court was largely concerned with improving the fences and enclosures in the park. He also built a new lodge there.

In such projects he was doubtless encouraged by his Queen. Anne of Denmark shared her husband's enthusiasm for the chase. Ben Jonson flatteringly called her 'the Huntress Queen', and there is, in the royal collection, a fine portrait of her in hunting apparel, her greyhounds about her feet. Although she cut a better figure than her husband did, her skill was perhaps even more suspect than his. On one occasion she 'mistook her mark' and, missing the stag, shot 'the King's more principal and special hound', Jewel. The King, when he heard of the dog's death, 'stormed exceedingly'. But, learning that it was his Queen who had fired the arrow, he relented and the next day sent her 'a diamond worth £2,000 as a legacy from his dead dog'.

Beyond hunting, the Queen's great love was drama. The plays and masques performed at court under Queen Elizabeth were continued and amplified. King James spent his first Christmas at Hampton Court. The courtiers and their servants banded together to put on some thirty productions. The most splendid of these was *The Vision of the Twelve Goddesses*, a masque commissioned by the Queen from the poet Samuel Daniel. The Queen herself appeared as Pallas Athena, the other goddesses and graces being personified by noble ladies of the court. Queen Elizabeth's wardrobe was opened up to provide fantastical costumes. The scenery included, at the lower end of the hall, a vast mountain and, at the upper end, a 'Temple of Peace' and a 'Cave of Sleep'. These sets were probably designed by Inigo Jones who had recently returned from Denmark where he had been at the court of the Queen's brother, King Christian IV. Certainly he became the principal designer for the royal masques in later years, and – from 1615 – the Surveyor of the King's Buildings.

If Inigo Jones were present that Christmas he was part of an extraordinary gathering of talent. Amongst the various troupes performing was the recently instituted 'King's Company of Comedians'. On New Year's night they acted *Robin Goodfellow* in the Great Hall. One of the leading actors was William Shakespeare. And it is more than possible that one of Shakespeare's own plays was included amongst the six that the company put on that Christmas.

Another of the period's great literary achievements had an even closer association with the palace. In the immediate wake of the Christmas festivities of 1603/4, the King summoned a Conference to Hampton Court to discuss the grievances of the Puritan party within the Church of England. He had received a petition listing some of these complaints with over a thousand signatures. Although the King dismissed most of the points brought forward by the four-man Puritan delegation, one he did take up. Dr John Reynolds, the Puritan President of Corpus Christi College, Oxford, in his address to the Council, ventured the suggestion, 'May your Majesty be pleased that the Bible be new translated, such translations as are extant not answering the original?'

Although one of the Anglican bishops hastened to ridicule the idea, the King stopped him. He took up the theme himself: 'I wish,' he declared, 'some special plans were taken for a uniform translation, which should be done by the best learned in both universities, then reviewed by the bishops, presented to the Privy Council, and lastly ratified by royal authority to be read in the whole church, and no other.' This lucidly laid out instruction marked the origin of the Authorized Version of the Bible in English, one of the golden books of English prose.

Although King James was often a reluctant host he did when necessary use the palace to impress important foreign dignitaries. They seem to have responded to the magic of the place, none more so than the Queen's brother, King Christian, who visited during the summer of 1605. A day's hunting was followed by a night of truly Scandinavian revelry. One of the English courtiers gave the following account of what he could remember of the night's festivities. 'We had women and wine too of such plenty as would have astonished each beholder. Our feasts were magnificent and the royal guests did most lovingly embrace each other at the table. I think the Dane hath strangely wrought on our good English nobles: for those whom I could never get to taste good English liquor now follow the fashion and wallow in beastly delights. The ladies abandon their sobriety and are seen to roll about in intoxication.'

King James, though keen on wine, was less interested in women. As his reign advanced he fell increasingly under the thrall of his male favourites. He conceived passionate attachments to a succession of young men, heaping them with presents and offices. His abiding love was George Villiers, whom he made the Duke of Buckingham and the Secretary of State. Nevertheless, despite these homosexual infatuations, he retained a real affection for his Queen. He was much concerned with her declining health. Early in 1619, when she fell seriously ill, he had her brought to Hampton Court. The air there seemed to suit her well. She was suffering from tuberculosis, gout and dropsy. The move seemed to have a tonic effect. As one of the ladies-in-waiting recorded: 'She was reasonably well recovered to the eyes of all that saw her, and came to her drawing chamber and to her gallery every day almost; yet still so weak of her legs that she could not stand upon them, neither had she any stomach for her meat, the space of six weeks before she died.... On the 22nd of February she took a flux [cough] vehemently, which she has had all this winter, which is now seen to be the cough of the lungs by a consumption.'

By the beginning of March her condition was critical. James himself was ill in London, but much of the court travelled out to the palace. According to one eyewitness account, 'she lay so pleasantly in the bed smiling, as if she had no pain; only, in the last, she gave five or six little groans, and had the pleasantest going out of this world that ever anybody had; and two days after looked as well as she did at any time this two years.' She died, it was said, just as the palace clock struck four in the morning. And, according to tradition, the clock has since that time always stopped when a death occurs in the palace. The King had himself painted in 'a melancholy suit of solemn black' by the court artist Van Somer.

Although James I appointed Inigo Jones as the Surveyor of the King's Buildings, the great architect made no contribution to the structure of Hampton Court. Perhaps there were plans to do something: on the flyleaf of a volume of Palladio's sketches which once belonged to him, Jones jotted down the dimensions of the palace's principal courtyards: 'The first Court of Hampton Court is 166 fo. square. The Second Fountaine Court is 92 fo. broade, and 150 fo. longe. The Greene Court is 108 fo. broade, and 116 fo. longe, the walkes or cloysters ar 14 fo. betweene walles.'

Jones, nevertheless, did maintain an interest in the palace. One of his letters relates to a visit he made. He wrote to the Earl of Arundel:

In my journey to London I went to Hampton Court, where I heard that the Spanish ambassador came to Kingston and sent his steward to Hampton Court, who looked on the lodgings intended for the ambassador, which were in Mr Huggins his rooms; but the steward utterly disliked those rooms, saying that the ambassador would not lie but in the house (meaning the Palace); besides there was no furniture in those rooms, or bedding, or otherwise, neither for the ambassador or his followers. So the steward returning to his lord, he resolved only to hunt in the park and so return. But the Keeper answered he might not suffer that, he having received no order for it; so the ambassador went back discontented, having had some smart sport at the warren. But since, my lord of Nottingham hearing of this, sent to the ambassador to excuse the matter, which the ambassador took very well and promised to come and lie at Hampton Court before His Majesty's return.

The King was anxious to win the favour of the Spanish ambassador. He was hoping to marry Prince Charles to the Infanta Maria, daughter of the King of Spain. The plan, however, came to nothing. Negotiations were then opened with Louis XIII of France. It was proposed that Charles should marry the King's sister, Henrietta Maria. Matters were still being discussed when James I died in March 1625.

The King's Beasts guarding the palace gate.

THE FLOWER SHOW

Over the centuries every visitor to Hampton Court has marvelled at the palace gardens and their flowers: the intricate knots of Wolsey's time, the chequerboard motifs of the later Tudors, the formal patterns of the Stuarts, the bizarre 'Exoticks' gathered by William and Mary, the naturalistic arrangements of the Georgians, and the riotous colour of the Victorian beds and borders. Since 1990 this floribundant tradition has been carried forward into new and exciting areas by the Hampton Court Flower Show.

Since 1994, the event has been organized by the Royal Horticultural Society, and, under the society's auspices, has grown to be the largest flower show in the country. It is bigger, more popular and more accessible than even the Chelsea Flower Show. It takes place over a week in July.

The setting is spectacular. The showground is situated in the Home Park, just beyond the semi-circular canal at the end of the Fountain Gardens, on a site running up beside the Long Water canal. The whole area is turned into a glorious patchwork of show gardens and plant plots. The proximity of the Long Water allows for the inclusion of water gardens and water features.

The Hampton Court Flower Show also plays host to the British Rose Festival. So, each year, there is a fabulous array of roses – the living floral symbols of the Tudor royal house.

The 'Garden of the Spirit' at the 1998 show.

Almost overnight a vast encampment of pavilions, marquees and stands springs up to accommodate the 800 exhibitors. Each year the show attracts some 200,000 visitors.

Installing the vast encampment – and providing access for the visitors – is a logistical operation of almost military proportions. Although much of the organization is in the hands of the Royal Horticultural Society, on the palace side the control of the great undertaking falls largely on the shoulders of Graham Dillamore, Hampton Court's Deputy Gardener.

He admits with relief that the task, although problematic, is not quite as difficult as it might be. At least the whole event takes place outside the palace itself. There is not the constant anxiety – as there is with the music festival arrangements in Base Court – that contractors will inadvertently damage the historic fabric of the building with a stray piece of scaffolding or an unattended light fixture.

Nevertheless there are other worries to contend with. Graham is always anxious that the traditional inhabitants of the Home Park – the fallow deer – are not inconvenienced or distressed more than is absolutely necessary. The Flower Show area itself is cordoned off, but the deer are given a free run in the rest of the park.

If setting up the show is a major operation, dismantling it is even more fraught. Traditionally it ends on the Sunday afternoon with a frantic one-hour sell-off of most of the plants and

products on display. Then, after, the plant-laden public has been ushered from the site, the contractors strive to dismantle and remove all the stands and tents by half past ten that evening. The task is rarely assisted by the caprices of the English summer weather.

Despite the best efforts of all the exhibitors and the Royal Horticultural Society the scene left by the departing hoards is one of devastation: flattened, colourless grass and mud. Although the Flower Show lasts only seven days, Terry Gough, the Head Gardener, estimates that the site takes almost a year

LEFT The Show attracts thousands of visitors to Hampton Court. BELOW Elaborate gardens are constructed almost overnight.

to recover from the impact. The garden staff charged with co-ordinating the event probably take about the same time.

In its glory, however, the show ground presents a magical sight. The myriad tents and marquees are reminiscent of the times when great retinues of foreign ambassadors and princes had to be accommodated under canvas and vast, tented encampments were set up in the park.

The Flower Show, moreover, also forges other, less expected but more practical, links with the palace's history. The gardening team has discovered that the old Tudor culverts running across the park make ideal sewers for the temporary lavatories. At Hampton Court the past and the present are always making unexpected connections.

SECURITY

At Hampton Court security has always been a challenge. The palace is so vast that it is difficult to monitor or patrol. From the days of Cardinal Wolsey there have been constant complaints about pilfering and worse. One Christmas, during the reign of Elizabeth I, the festivities were interrupted when it was discovered that four 'gentlemen pensioners' who were quartered in one of the Tilt Yard towers had been robbed. As the contemporary account states, 'at six o'clock at night their chamber door… was broken open, and all their trunks likewise, out of all of which the thieves took and carried away of jewels and ready money from these four, to the value of £400.' A thorough search of the vicinity was made, and the principal delinquent discovered. He was subsequently hanged.

The largest and most delicate security operation at Hampton Court, however, was concerned not with preventing thieves from breaking in but with preventing a King from breaking out. After his defeat in the Civil War, Charles I was held prisoner at Hampton Court by the Parliamentary forces. He was treated with the greatest respect by his gaolers. No especial guards were set on him. He was allowed the run of the palace, was able to receive visitors, and was even permitted to go hunting in the park.

The Great Doors of the palace are closed at the end of each day.

On the morning of Thursday 11 November he shut himself in his bedchamber, ostensibly to write letters as was his custom. He knew that he would not be disturbed until five or six in the late afternoon. As soon as darkness began to fall, which it did early, he left his room on the south side of Cloister Green Court, accompanied by his faithful friend Colonel Legge. They proceeded to the end of the King's Long Gallery, went down a small staircase and then gained the cover of the Water Gallery. At the water's edge two other friends were waiting with a boat to take the King across the river and horses to carry him to the coast.

The escape was made undetected. At half-past five the guards did knock at the King's door, but getting no answer they waited. They spent a great deal of time outside that door, none of them daring to knock it down. Even in captivity the King was able to project an aura of majesty. Although Charles got safely away from Hampton Court, he did not get very much further. He reached the Isle of Wight before being recaptured, and was taken first to Windsor and then to London. He was executed on 30 January 1649.

In recent times the security concerns of Hampton Court have been less momentous. When the general public was first let into the palace in 1838 there was much anxiety that the building would swiftly be stripped of its treasures. Ernest Law recalled the 'gloomy prognostications' of the time: 'Visions of an insulting rabble, such as that

which invaded the Tuileries in the time of Louis XVI, marching through the State Apartments, tearing down the tapestries, wrecking the furniture, and carrying off the pictures, seemed to arise in the terrified imagination of some.'

Such anxieties have not, however, been fulfilled. Nevertheless, Dennis McGuinnes, the palace's Deputy Director, still maintains a close watch on all security matters. 'Like everything else,' he admits, 'technology is racing on. There is always pressure to get the latest equipment. But you have to balance that against the expense. We had some security consultants come in to look over the palace. Their recommendations stopped short of machine-gun emplacements on the roof, but only just. We would have had to sell the collection to pay for all their measures!'

Electronic technology is certainly useful, but it has to be backed up with human vigilance and sound procedures. 'We have to accept that people will watch us,' explains McGuinnes, who is a former Metropolitan Police officer. 'I am always stressing that to the warders.' His warnings were confirmed recently when there was an armed robbery of a security van just over the Hampton Court Bridge. The van's last call had been at the palace…

The inside of the palace is carefully monitored. There are over 250 intruder alarms *in situ*, all of them linked to a central control room. Nevertheless, the human element in the security equation remains strong. The alarm system is backed up by a team of security warders providing round-the-clock patrols.

The night shift can get a bit spooky, as Kevin Coates, one of the guards admits. 'It's a bit eerie to say the least,' Kevin confesses. All sorts of

Kevin Coates on his rounds.

Dennis McGuinnes takes an overall view.

unexpected phenomena can prove unsettling. 'There are times when you're walking along and you hit a hot spot, or suddenly it goes cold. Sometimes there is a smell of perfume, which disappears when you take a step forward. But then – when you step back – it's there again…'

Happily, perhaps, the guards are obliged to be in constant radio contact with the control room. Every time a guard passes through an area that activates an alarm, he radios his position through.

The actual duties of a night security guard tend to be quite mundane. 'We check through all the apartments and offices that are in use,' explains Coates, 'looking out for any signs of damage. We look out for taps left running or lights left on.' Something as trivial as a plug left in a basin with a dripping tap can have serious consequences. 'The trouble is that this is a historic palace, not just a domestic situation, so any accident – however small – can cost "big money".'

CHAPTER 4

THE PALACE REVIVED

The marriage of Charles I and Henrietta Maria took place soon after King James's funeral, and Hampton Court was the scene of the royal honeymoon. The new King was in his early twenties, his bride was just fifteen. Both were diminutive, fine-featured and highly strung. They had, personally, much in common, but the demands and constrictions of court protocol obscured the fact. Dynastic marriages were not intimate affairs. The new Queen arrived in England with a train of over a hundred people. She brought her own Lord Chamberlain, the Comte de Tillières, two ambassadors, a bishop, thirty Roman Catholic priests (for she was allowed to continue in her own religion), a confessor, a bevy of ladies-in-waiting and numerous general servants and retainers. This large retinue served to cocoon the Queen from her new subjects, from

OPPOSITE Hendrick Danckert's seventeenth-century painting of the palace. ABOVE The Long Water.

the court, and even from her husband. It gave her no encouragement to learn her new language.

But the situation was made worse. Of the ladies-in-waiting one in particular exercised a powerful influence over the Queen. Henrietta Maria would do nothing without consulting Madame de Saint-Georges, who had – since childhood – been her companion and confidante. It was a relationship that the King came quickly to resent. He made what effort he could to break it. For the journey down from London to Hampton Court he dismissed the large coach that had been prepared and travelled in a much smaller vehicle, which had room only for himself, his bride and two others. He made sure that these two places were taken by his own courtiers. If the Queen did not perceive the snub to Madame de Saint-Georges, Madame de Saint-Georges soon informed her of it. And the Queen passed on her resentment to the King.

Charles I, like his father, relied upon the counsel of the Duke of Buckingham. The Duke was despatched to the Queen's chambers to effect a solution. The interview was not a success. Buckingham, with rather more severity than tact, told the Queen that she was failing in her duty to her husband and that she must break off her attachment to Madame de Saint-Georges at once. The Queen refused to be drawn. The following day Buckingham changed tack. Adopting a strategy of infiltration rather than confrontation, he asked whether the Queen might honour him by appointing his own wife, sister and niece as Ladies of the Bedchamber. The Queen, however, politely demurred. She explained that she had brought her own ladies with her from France. Nevertheless she agreed to discuss the question with the ambassador.

Buckingham then tried to outmanoeuvre her by taking up the matter himself with the ambassador, suggesting to him that the arrangement would be beneficial not only to the Queen but also to France. They consulted with the Queen's bishop. But he dismissed the idea out of hand, claiming that it would be dangerous to expose the young Queen to the heretical influence of non-Catholic companions in her own Bedchamber. Again Buckingham and the King were confounded.

The tension between the two factions continued to simmer. It found a vent when the court prepared to move on from Hampton Court to Windsor. The King was much exercised with how he might separate the Queen from Madame de Saint-Georges for the journey. He discussed the matter with Buckingham, who suggested the expedient of taking the small coach again and inviting two English ladies to ride with them. Madame de Saint-Georges, however, was prepared. She was determined not to be denied a second time. As the royal party made ready to drive off, she attempted to climb into the coach. The King at once lent

forward, seized her arm, and pushed her back. It was altogether a very ignominious incident. The Queen was much upset. So was the King. The drive to Windsor must have seemed very long.

The court soon returned to Hampton Court. The travel arrangements are unrecorded but already other areas of conflict were making themselves apparent. The Queen's Catholicism became a growing source of division. On one occasion when the royal couple were dining in state in the Presence Chamber, one of the court chaplains was about to say grace when Father Bérulle, the Queen's confessor, interposed with a grace of his own. An unsightly scuffle broke out as the two priests jostled for position while trying to drown each other out. The King ignored the incident and began the meal without waiting for either prelate to finish. When the same charade threatened to be repeated at the end of the dinner, he 'instantly rose from the table' and 'in a great passion...taking the Queen by the hand, retired to the bedchamber'.

Such private disputes, however, became more public when the Queen refused to be crowned with the King at Westminster Abbey. Her objections were religious but the snub was keenly resented by the English. The King, exasperated by the constant tensions of his domestic position, resolved on drastic action. He instructed Buckingham to expel all the Queen's retainers at once and without delay: 'If you can by fair means (but strike not long in disputing), otherways, force them away, dryving them lyke so manie wylde beastes, until ye have shipped them, and so the Devill goe with them.' After the expulsion the King's household were shocked to discover that the retainers had carried off all the Queen's trousseau with them. Some delicate diplomacy was called for. The Maréchal de Bassompierre was despatched from France.

The King was once more in residence at Hampton Court. The Maréchal was brought there at once in one of the King's coaches. Measures had been taken to make him welcome. An elaborate dinner had been prepared. But, perhaps deliberately, he arrived too late to eat it. A more modest supper was offered to him but this too he declined. Buckingham then called and asked what he proposed to say to the King. Bassompierre replied haughtily that he would deliver his messages to the King in person or not at all. Buckingham was obliged to explain that the King wanted to know in advance the purport of Bassompierre's mission because he feared that any discussion of the dismissal of the Queen's servants would put him in such 'a passion' that he might 'commit some extravagance and cry in sight of everybody'.

Bassompierre must have been able to offer some reassurance. The next day he was formally received in the Presence Chamber, the King and Queen sitting beneath the cloth of estate, the court in attendance. 'The Company was magnificent,' he recorded, 'the order exquisite. I made my compliment to the King, gave him my letters and said my words of civility.' That was the limit of public audience.

Four days later the ambassador had a private interview with the King in one of the galleries. This was not such a sedate affair. The King worked himself into a 'great passion', rehearsed all his old complaints about the Queen's French retainers and concluded his outburst by asking Bassompierre why he did not 'execute [his] commission at once and declare war'.

Bassompierre assured him that was not the French intention. The King calmed down. A few minor concessions were mapped out and agreed.

Charles I and Henrietta Maria with their two eldest children, by Sir Anthony van Dyck.

The Queen was allowed to have two Catholic priests, and three women attendants who could speak French, although these were to be chosen by the King.

In the wake of Bassompierre's diplomatic embassy, relations between Charles and his Queen began to improve. Their intimacy was further increased when Buckingham was killed in August 1628. The Queen gave birth to her first child in May 1629, and although the baby died within the hour, a second son was born the next year. Seven other children followed.

The unhappy memories of the honeymoon soon faded and Hampton Court became one of the royal couple's favoured residences. They visited it two or three times each year. The Queen, like her predecessor, delighted in theatrical entertainments. The Great Hall was in frequent use as a theatre. The Queen herself acted in many productions, and she watched even more.

She is said to have decorated her apartments, although nothing survives of her schemes. Charles's legacy has been more enduring. As a young man he had – during an embassy to the Spanish court – developed a love for paintings. He had commissioned Velázquez to paint his portrait and his interest had been acknowledged and encouraged by the Spanish King, who presented him with 'four raire' paintings by Tintoretto when he returned home.

His taste was a novel one. In England tapestry was still regarded as the pre-eminent medium for great art. When Charles became King he was able to indulge his interest more fully. He began to collect and to commission. Many important artists were invited to England to work. Rubens was brought over to paint the ceiling of the new Banqueting House at Whitehall, Van Dyck produced a ceaseless stream of exquisite royal portraits. Charles's agents scoured Italy for works by the masters of the Italian Renaissance. He

Esther before Ahasuerus by Tintoretto, one of Charles I's prized acquisitions.

The Holy Family *by Dosso Dossi, bought by Charles I from the Gonzaga collection.*

bought paintings by Titian, Giorgione, Correggio and the Carracci. Perhaps his greatest coup was to secure much of the collection assembled by the Gonzaga Duke of Mantua.

Of the many, many pictures that King Charles acquired, nearly 400 were hung at Hampton Court. They must have radically altered the aspect of the palace. Amongst the works was the great series of *The Triumphs of Caesar* – nine canvases by Andrea Mantegna which can still be seen at the palace.

Charles's enthusiasm for works of art was by no means confined to painting. He bought curiosities, jewels and ivories. He imported furniture from the Continent. He set up classical statues in the palace gardens. He also commissioned an extravagant fountain of marble and bronze from the Italian artist Francesco Fanelli. It was to represent the goddess Arethusa, surrounded by a riot of boys, dolphins and sirens with spouting breasts. He installed it in the Privy Garden.

The King made only one alteration to the fabric of the palace: he built a new covered tennis court, at the far northeastern angle of the palace buildings (which still survives today). He also effected a minor change in the park. In 1638 he instituted a scheme to divert a tributary of the nearby Colne River across Hounslow Heath and into Bushy Park. The new waterway, called the Longford River, provided a useful additional water supply, not only for the park and gardens but also for the palace. The cutting of the channel provoked much opposition from those whose land it crossed on its way into the park.

Even louder complaints greeted the news of the King's other grand plan. Following the loss of Henry VIII's great chase, he wanted to enclose a vast stretch of land between Hampton Court and Richmond, to make his own new Royal Hunting Chase. He ignored the petitions of outraged farmers and landowners, and was only dissuaded from the controversial scheme at the last moment by the intercession of the Archbishop of Canterbury.

The plan, however, was characteristic of the King's high-handedness. It was a trait which was drawing him into ever-increasing conflict with Parliament and drawing the country towards the cataclysm of civil war.

In the winter of 1641 Parliament drew up a list of its chief complaints against the King's government and its recommendations for the future. This 'Grand Remonstrance' was presented to the King at Hampton Court on 1 December. Charles was much distressed by its length and the powerful language in which it was written. He promised to answer it 'as soon as the weight of business would permit', but he 'desired there should be no publishing' of the declaration until he had had time to answer it. Parliament ignored the request and 'blazoned' the document 'throughout the Kingdom'.

The situation deteriorated quickly. Charles returned to London and made his ill-fated attempt

A view of the palace from the river showing Charles I and his sons in their boat.

to enter the House of Commons and arrest five of his most vociferous critics. Parliamentary and popular opinion in the capital rose up against him. In alarm he fled with his family back to Hampton Court, escorted by Colonel Lunsford and 200 men. Such was the haste of their flight that no proper preparation had been made to receive him. The King and Queen, together with their three eldest children – Charles, Prince of Wales, James, Duke of York, and Mary – were obliged to sleep together in one room.

Civil war had become inevitable. As an opening gambit Charles's removal to Hampton Court was disastrous. London was surrendered into the hands of the Parliamentarians without a fight. Although Colonel Lunsford rode over to Kingston to secure the arsenal there, Hampton Court itself was (as Edward VI had discovered) unsuitable as a refuge. After a few days the King moved on to the greater safety of Windsor Castle. The King would return to Hampton Court five years later as a prisoner.

BOUGHT AND SOLD

The palace remained largely undisturbed during the Civil War, at least until 1645. Following the Battle of Naseby it was taken over by the Parliamentary forces. The State Apartments were left intact and sealed, but the Chapel provoked the iconoclastic ire of the Puritan faction. As a contemporary broadsheet recorded:

Sir Robert Harlow gave order for the putting down and demolishing of the popish and superstitious pictures at Hampton Court, where this day the altar was taken down and the table brought into the body of the church, the rails pulled down, and the steps levelled, and the popish and superstitious images that were in the glass windows were also demolished, and an order was given for the new glazing them with plain glass; and among the rest, there was pulled down the picture of Christ nailed to the cross, which was right over the altar and the pictures of Mary Magdalen and others weeping by the foot of the cross, and some other such idolatrous pictures were pulled down and demolished.

After the regicide of Charles I, the Commonwealth was uncertain what to do with Hampton Court. Parliament's first instinct was to sell off everything belonging to the Crown and a bill was duly passed to this effect on 4 July 1649. Inventories were made of all the Royal Palaces with estimates of the prices. Amongst the tapestries were such choice lots as 'Ten pieces of rich Arras of Joshuah at £3,399; nine pieces of Tobias at £3,409; nine pieces of Arras of St. Paule at £3,065'. The paintings were valued very much lower: Titian's *Herodias with the Head of John the Baptist* was priced at only £150, and even his highly regarded *Madonna del Pardo* was set at a mere £600. The whole set of Mantegna's *Triumphs of Caesar* could have been got for £1,000.

The inventory also gives a picture of the great accumulation of royal bric-à-brac gathered at the palace. Amongst the curiosities listed are Henry VIII's cane (value: five shillings) and a pair of his gloves (value: one shilling). The palace itself was valued with extraordinary niceness at £7,777 13 shillings and 5 pence, the parks at £10,765 19 shillings and 9 pence.

The estimates, however, were not immediately put to the trial of auction. The following year the Council of State exempted Hampton Court, together with the palaces of Whitehall and Westminster, from the general sale. Many of the more important tapestries, pictures, hangings and 'distinguished works of art and curiosity' were also withdrawn, and reserved 'for the use of the Commonwealth'.

In 1651, after the defeat of Charles II at Worcester terminated the brief episode of the Second Civil War, the Council of State had a suite of rooms at the palace prepared to receive the victorious Oliver Cromwell. He had, apparently, expressed a liking for the place. Cromwell's tenure, however, was soon brought into doubt. Some elements within Parliament were anxious to strip the last of the royal assets. At the end of 1652 the House of Commons reversed its decision not to sell Hampton Court. This, however, was not the end of it. As a compromise it was suggested to Cromwell that he should *buy* the place. He refused, unwilling to assume the dignity of so magnificent a palace. His supporters seem to have been only partially convinced by this modest refusal. It was resolved to keep the palace but to sell off the parks. They duly went under the auctioneer's hammer.

A month later, however, the situation changed again when Cromwell was proclaimed Lord Protector of the Commonwealth. As the setting for a Head of State, Hampton Court was considered entirely appropriate. The decision was reversed yet again. The land was bought back by the Commonwealth for £2,000 more than had been paid for it. The palace and grounds were then presented to Cromwell.

Cromwell spent much time at Hampton Court over the coming years. His life there mimicked, after a more homely fashion, that of the monarchs who had preceded him. The Lord Protector took over the King's Lodgings, though it is not known whether his wife, the Lady Protectress, resided in the Queen's Lodgings. Although he was a man of simple, even severe, habits, Cromwell came from the prosperous landed gentry. His great-great uncle was Thomas Cromwell, who had succeeded Thomas More as Henry VIII's Chancellor. Great houses were not completely strange to him.

Cromwell was a strict Puritan in religion, but in his domestic life he seems to have allowed a certain amount of gaiety and colour. His behaviour at family gatherings was often rumbustious. On one occasion he caused general merriment by throwing about 'the sack posset amongst all the ladies to spoil their clothes, which they took as a favour, and daubed all the stools where they were to sit, with wet sweet-meats'.

He was also capable of refinement. He was fond of music, and had two organs installed in the Great Hall. It is said that his secretary, the poet John Milton, would sometimes play to him there. He himself was known to entertain the company after dinner with a psalm. He appreciated the arts sufficiently to admire Mantegna's *Triumphs of Caesar* (or perhaps it was the pictures' stern warning about the corruptibility of victorious republicanism that appealed to his moral sense). He had the series moved to the Long Gallery where he took his exercise. He preserved, too, many of the best tapestries from Henry VIII's great collection, decorating the Hall and State Apartments with them. Nor did he confine his choice to those dealing with biblical themes. In his own bedchamber he hung 'five tapestry hangings of Vulcan and Venus'.

The other furnishings of his bedchamber are listed in the inventory made after his death. They create an interesting picture of his taste in home decoration: 'two window curtains, one of scarlet baize, the other of serge; one small couch of fly-coloured damask, cased with watchet baize; two elbow chairs ditto; four black stools ditto; one black table with a turned frame'.

Within this baize environment Cromwell was almost always at work. Whenever he made an extended visit to Hampton Court his Council was in attendance. On rare occasions he even provided official entertainment at the palace. The Swedish ambassador was accorded the honour of a banquet there on 26 July 1656. The form and ceremonial of the dinner followed the plan of the former royal banquets.

For the most part, however, his style of living was simple. Both modes of life inevitably provoked his critics to satire. His frugality was called meanness, and his attempts at courtliness were condemned as ridiculous and hypocritical. As one hostile witness recounted, 'A great deal of State was now used towards him; and the *French* Cringe, and other ceremonious pieces of gallantry and good

A panel from Mantegna's Triumphs of Caesar.

deportment, which were thought unchristian and savouring of carnality, introduced in place of austere and down-cast looks, and silent mummery of starched and hypocritical gravity, the only becoming dress, forsooth, of Piety and Religion.'

Cromwell's wife – 'Old Joan' as she was ungraciously called – was a particular butt of the royalist wits. Her close domestic economy was especially derided. It was claimed that she had employed a surveyor to make a network of passages and trapdoors throughout the palace, 'By which she might at all times, unseen, pass to and fro, and come unawares upon her servants, and keep them vigilant in their places'.

Cromwell himself took great pleasure in his wife and family. His children were often around him at Hampton Court. Most of them had designated rooms in the palace. Two of his daughters were married in the Chapel. Indeed one of them was married there twice. Mary Cromwell, the Protector's third daughter, to please her father, went through a Puritan rite of marriage in the morning and then – later in the same day – to please herself, was married again 'according to the form prescribed by the Church of England'.

Another of Cromwell's daughters died at the palace, after a short illness. The Protector spent much time at her bedside. According to royalist propaganda she raved a great deal in her fever, reproaching her father for his regicide and urging him to atone.

Although Cromwell disapproved of tennis and other sports, he enjoyed hunting in the park. He seems to have been more accommodating to the local hunt followers than the early Stuart monarchs: sometimes 'to coax the neighbouring rusticks' he would present them with a buck 'and money to drink with it'. In other respects, however, he seems to have been just as careless of local opinion.

The one piece of building work that he undertook at Hampton Court was not calculated to please his neighbours. He restored the flow of King Charles's Longford River. The local inhabitants had always resented the new river because of its tendency to flood their fields. They had taken the opportunity of the Civil War to dam it up, breaking down the footbridges into the stream, and tipping in cartloads of gravel. Cromwell, whatever his views had been on King Charles's political rule, was a keen admirer of the old King's landscape gardening. He set about rebuilding the bridges, mending the banks and dredging the bottom. He even extended the stream further eastward into Bushy Park, making two small lakes in the area known as the Hare Warren. One of these is known today as the Heron Pond. Herons do, indeed, sometimes alight there, but the name is a corruption of its original designation: the Hare Warren pond.

Cromwell lived in constant danger of assassination. Embittered royalists, and even discontented members of his own party, wished him dead. He took to wearing a chain-mail undershirt at all times. It is said that, in order to foil ambushers, he never took the same route from London to Hampton Court twice. One would-be assassin did manage to gain entry into the palace. Captain Thomas Gardiner was arrested in a gallery at Hampton Court with two loaded pistols and a dagger. He was imprisoned for twelve months but escaped the hangman due to 'want of evidence'. After the Restoration he applied to the King for a pension.

The constant anxiety about attack had a debilitating effect upon Cromwell's health. In the late summer of 1658 he fell seriously ill at Hampton Court. Although his doctors despaired, Cromwell himself was convinced that through prayer he might recover. He convinced others too. A public fast was 'ordered for his sake, and kept at Hampton Court...to pray to God for his health, as they thanked him for the undoubted pledges of his recovery'. The pledges, however, proved quite unfounded. Cromwell's condition worsened. He was moved to Whitehall for a change of air, but to no avail. He died on 2 September.

Cromwell's son, Richard, succeeded as Lord Protector, but the arrangement soon proved unworkable. The great office was far too heavy a burden for the amiable but indolent 'Tumbledown

Dick'. Power soon returned to Parliament. The national exchequer was in a bad condition. Money had to be raised. It was proposed that the contents of Hampton Court and the other state-owned palaces, at Whitehall and St James's, might be sold off. There was, however, a difficulty about the scheme: the Cromwell family claimed that much of the furniture and art at Hampton Court was no longer government property but had been bought by the late Lord Protector. Although the point was disputed, Mrs Cromwell took the initiative. She spirited away numerous pieces and hid them in a fruiterer's warehouse nearby.

There was further debate over what to do with the house itself. Some favoured selling it outright, not only to raise funds but also to prevent it from becoming a temptation to ambitious men, sharpening 'their appetite to ascend the Throne'. General Ludlow thought that the palace would make an excellent rest home for 'those that were employed in public affairs when they should be indisposed in the summer season'. With the emergence of General Monk as the commanding political figure of the hour it was next decided to offer the palace to him. Monk, however, was working secretly to achieve the Restoration of the monarchy and was thus reluctant to accept anything more than the 'custody and stewardship' of the palace.

THE PALACE RESTORED

Charles II was proclaimed King while still in exile. He returned to England on 29 May 1660, and was received with joyful enthusiasm by the nation. The 'Merry Monarch' was thirty years old. He seemed to be the antithesis of the doughty Puritans who had governed before him. Dark-haired, sallow-skinned, full-lipped, he ushered in an age of sensuous gaiety – at least at court. He surrounded himself with beautiful mistresses and extravagant wits. Although, as a country residence, the new King preferred Windsor, as a setting for pleasure, he recognized the charms of Hampton Court. His visits there, though brief, were not infrequent.

He redecorated the rooms, restored the furnishings and recovered the furniture from Mrs Cromwell's warehouse. Amongst the small additions he made to the palace decor were two impressive iron firebacks, still at Hampton Court. They were wrought with the King's adopted emblem, 'The Royal Oak', a reminder of how he evaded his pursuers after the Battle of Worcester by hiding in an oak tree. Charles had at one time considered instituting an 'Order of the Royal Oak' as a grand memorial of the event but, in the end, he lowered his sights to domestic ironmongery.

The King also looked beyond the small details of furnishing. He was the first monarch since Henry VIII to show an enthusiasm for ambitious construction schemes at Hampton Court. His exile on the Continent had introduced him to new and modish ideas about architecture and landscape gardening. He lost little time in putting them into practice. At Hampton Court he conceived a 'Grand Design' for the gardens. He wanted something in the latest French style.

Instead of the enclosed, intricately planted designs of earlier English gardens, he proposed a more open, spacious and majestic arrangement. From a grand semi-circular area in front of the eastern range of the palace, three evenly spaced vistas were to radiate out towards the distant curve of the Thames. The effect was that of a giant 'goose foot', or *patte d'oie* as it was called by the French gardeners who directed the scheme. Charles had hoped to persuade Louis XIV's innovative garden-designer, André Le Nôtre, to work on the plan. But although Le Nôtre did lay out a parterre for the Queen's House at Greenwich, it seems unlikely that he contributed anything specific to the Hampton Court scheme. The design was probably developed by Le Nôtre's mentor, André Mollet. Certainly Mollet had commended the notion of a three-toed 'goose foot' radiating from a double semi-circle of trees in his influential book, *Le Jardin de plaisir*. The central 'toe' in Charles's Hampton

The original semi-circular plan of Charles II's garden is still visible.

Court design was a long canal, flanked by a double row of lime trees. The 'toes' on either side were broad avenues, also flanked with double lines of limes. The water for the canal – or 'Long Water' – was supplied by the Longford River. The lime trees came from Holland. By 1662 the work was almost completed. The diarist John Evelyn, visiting the park in June of that year, found it 'planted with sweet rows of lime trees, and the canal water now near perfected'.

King Charles's work on the fabric of the palace was more modest. He completely overhauled the tennis court lying at the north end of the Broadwalk, after its years of Puritan neglect. With great consideration for the spectators he supplied

all the seats with velvet cushions. The King, for his part, preferred to play rather than watch. He was even a good player. Pepys saw him on court once, but his pleasure in the game was vitiated by the way sycophantic courtiers would praise the King's bad shots as well as his good ones.

King Charles's other recreation was love. He loved women. He gathered beauties about him. He had, during his travels, enjoyed a succession of mistresses. He commissioned a series of portraits from the court artist, Peter Lely, depicting the most beautiful women of his court. Although the paintings were originally hung at Windsor, they have since been moved to Hampton Court. The array of bee-stung lips, heavy-lidded eyes and alabaster bosoms vividly conjures up the world of his court. Perhaps the most conspicuous of the Windsor Beauties was Barbara Palmer.

On his return to England the King took up this beautiful and well-born girl. She was the daughter of a cavalier who had died in the King's service. She was twenty and she was married. Her husband, however, was most complaisant. In acknowledgement of his good grace, Charles made him the Earl of Castlemaine. Despite the pleasures of this attachment – and sundry others – the King recognized that it was his duty to try to provide a legitimate heir.

Two years after returning to England, he married. His bride was the Portuguese princess Catherine of Braganza. He married her at Portsmouth immediately she disembarked from his ship and like his father, he brought his new bride to Hampton Court for the honeymoon. He had the palace specially prepared for her arrival. Sadly, nothing of his scheme of decoration has survived subsequent refurbishments. Nor is there any trace of the magnificent silver-and-crimson trimmed bed, the gift of the Dutch people, that was installed in the Queen's Bedchamber.

The royal couple arrived in great state, their carriage accompanied by a train of supporters. They were greeted by the assembled court. They then processed through the Great Hall and the State Apartments.

The Queen made a moderately favourable impression. Evelyn described her as 'though low of stature, prettily shaped, languishing and excellent eyes, her teeth wronging her mouth by sticking a little too far out: for the rest lovely enough'. But her chief merit seems to have been that she was not as ugly as her maids of honour. It was generally agreed that no more hideous entourage had ever arrived at court. The Comte de Grammont described them as 'six frights, who called themselves Maids of Honour, and a Duenna, another Monster, who took the title of governess to these extraordinary beauties'. Their lack of beauty, moreover, was matched by their lack of dress sense. Portuguese fashion currently favoured 'monstrous' farthingales, which appeared grotesque and cumbersome to English taste of the time.

The King had taken the precaution of getting his wife's measurements sent over from Portugal in advance so that he might commission a series of fashionable gowns for her. But she timidly refused to wear them. Charles did his best to ignore the fact. He tried to throw himself into the round of holiday pleasures. Evelyn gives an account of the royal couple boating on the Thames in a gondola sent to the King by the State of Venice, noting that the vessel was 'not comparable for swiftness to our common wherries, though managed by Venetians'. And on one evening he attended a recital of 'the Queen's Portugal music, consisting of fifes, harps, and very ill voices'.

But such conventional gaieties could not entirely capture the King's attention. Lady Castlemaine was staying in the palace. She had come there to give birth to the King's child. Once relieved of the baby she began a campaign to be installed as one of the Queen's ladies-in-waiting. The King found himself forced to agree to this rather inappropriate request, and put her name forward. The Queen, however, had been warned about her rival. She struck Lady Castlemaine's name from the list submitted to her. She refused to be introduced to her, or even to have her name mentioned.

A terrible struggle of wills ensued. The Queen was stubborn. Charles cajoled, bullied and intrigued. One day, unable to achieve his point by persuasion, he marched into the Queen's Presence Chamber with Lady Castlemaine. The Queen was there with her maids. Not knowing who Lady Castlemaine was, she rose to greet her. When she discovered that she had been tricked, she burst into tears, developed a nosebleed and then fainted.

The crisis once passed, however, things went more easily. The Queen changed her tactics. She not only admitted Lady Castlemaine to the Bedchamber, she made a friend and ally of her. The Countess in time achieved a recognized position as the King's mistress *en titre*. She was, it appears, initially lodged in the Water Gallery at the foot of the Privy Garden. Some alterations and improvements were carried out there during the 1660s. A balcony was added, looking out over the Thames, and the ground floor was fitted out as a miniature dairy, to provide milk for the royal table.

After his honeymoon, however, the King's own visits to Hampton Court were few and fleeting. He stopped there for a few weeks in 1665 when the plague was raging in London, before removing to the safer distance of Salisbury. And the following year, when the Great Fire devastated London, he sent many of his valuable pictures and objects down to Hampton Court for safekeeping.

In 1670, the year after he made Lady Castlemaine Duchess of Cleveland in her own right, King Charles added a wing to the southeast corner of the palace to provide a special suite of lodgings for her. Although the building was subsequently demolished, from the evidence of contemporary drawings it was built in the latest style, making few concessions to the existing Tudor structure. Also at this time the King prepared a set of apartments for his brother, James, Duke of York. He converted the old tennis court built by Henry VIII at the northeastern corner of the palace, and the lines of the Tudor building can still be seen in the well-fenestrated elevation of the elegant seventeenth-century range.

Although Charles II fathered five children by the Duchess of Cleveland he was unable to produce a legitimate heir. This became a matter of increasing anxiety. The Duke of York was next in line to the throne. He, however, had converted to Catholicism and was thus considered unacceptable. There were attempts to exclude him from the succession. Nevertheless, when Charles died in 1685 the matter was unresolved and James acceded to the throne.

It was a short reign. Despite his earlier association with the palace James II does not seem to have gone there as King. Apart from one recorded Council meeting that he held at Hampton Court, in May 1687 (and a cast-iron fireback with his arms on it) there is nothing to link him to the palace. His pro-Catholic policies soon incensed popular and political feeling. In 1688 Parliament invited James's daughter Mary, and her husband, William of Orange (who was the son of James's sister), to come and rule in his stead.

REAL TENNIS

*T*ennis has been a part of the life of Hampton Court since the time of Wolsey. It is still played at the palace in a form almost unaltered since the days of the Cardinal. It is now called 'real tennis' to distinguish it from the modern game of 'lawn tennis'. (It was only in the 1960s that *The Times* ceased referring to real tennis merely as 'tennis'. In Australia and Scotland it is called 'royal tennis', and in America 'court tennis'.)

From Tudor times the Keeper of the Tennis Play has had lodgings on site, at the north end of the court. And this arrangement persists today. Chris Ronaldson, the Keeper of the Royal Tennis Court, still lives in accommodation at the far end of the current court, together with his wife Lesley (who reached the top of the ladies' game) and their dynasty of tennis-playing sons. They are all keenly aware of being part of a great tradition. Both the court and the game have long and colourful histories.

The exact origins of the sport are obscure, concedes Lesley, who has made something of a study of the subject. There have been attempts to trace it back to the classical period. Certainly it had emerged as a popular pastime by the late Middle Ages. Initially it was played in the street. But as aristocratic enthusiasts took up the sport they began to build their own walled tennis courts – or 'plays'.

Tennis balls are still made by hand in the traditional way.

These were safer, more private and very much cleaner than the street of a medieval town. To preserve the flavour of the game, however, the architectural irregularities of the typical street – sloping roofs, tambours and windows – were built into the new courts as features.

The game prospered in the ducal and royal courts of Italy and France. And it found favour, too, in England, where it established itself as an important courtly diversion and accomplishment. Although rules and courts still varied from place to place there was a broad uniformity about the game: it was played with racquets, over a net in a walled court marked out with 'chases'. Both Edward IV and Henry VII had built plays at their palaces. Henry VIII built more. Wolsey, it seems, had already erected an open-air tennis play at Hampton Court. Henry built another, more up-to-date, covered one, on a site just beyond the northeast angle of the Chapel. It had large glazed windows with wire stretched over them for protection. This allowed Henry to indulge his enthusiasm for the sport, even when the weather was bad.

And the King was a very enthusiastic player, especially after he gave up jousting in 1530. He was also a good one. The Venetian ambassador to his court recorded that Henry was 'extremely fond of tennis, at which game it is the prettiest thing in the world to see him play, his fair skin glowing through a shirt of the finest texture'. The King wore special

Chris Ronaldson, Keeper of the Royal Tennis Court, and his wife, Lesley.

tennis slippers and drawers when playing. After the game he would don a black velvet 'tenys cote' to prevent himself catching a chill.

The royal accounts amply attest to Henry's love of tennis: there are payments to such figures as the man 'who served on the King's side at tennes at Hampton Court'. And there are frequent gambling debts owed to players and spectators. When the King was not playing himself, courtiers could hire the court for two shillings and sixpence a day.

The present tennis court, however, is not Henry VIII's. It was built in the late 1620s by Charles I, almost certainly on the site of Wolsey's original open-air play. The Stuarts were quite as fond of tennis as the Tudors. Charles I was not the only adept. His father, James I, played a match with the King of Denmark at Hampton Court. And Charles's older brother, Prince Henry, was regarded as a very skilful player before his early death in 1612. Charles I's tennis court was substantially refurbished and improved by Charles II following the Restoration. The roof was replaced, the floor was repaved and the penthouses were rebuilt. Charles also used the dimensions of the court to create an exact replica for his palace at Whitehall.

Henry VIII's old court, meanwhile, fell into disuse. Charles II adapted its basic fabric to make a set of lodgings for his sister-in-law, the Duchess of York. The buttresses of the old court can still be seen on this new building.

Since Charles II's time, the tennis court has endured its vicissitudes. During the construction of the new wing of the palace for William and Mary, Sir Christopher Wren used the space to store timber for almost a decade. When it was finally cleared, further restoration work was necessary. Amongst the various improvements a new stone floor was laid, replacing the old brick one. And it is William III's monogram that can still be seen on the main wall of the court today.

George I abandoned the tennis court altogether. He converted it into an additional drawing room during his brief attempt at sociability in 1718. He painted the walls white and converted the galleries for music. The court, however, was soon returned to use and some of the other Hanoverians showed an interest in the game.

Horace Walpole always claimed that the death of George II's eldest son, Frederick, Prince of Wales, was precipitated by a blow to the stomach from a tennis ball.

During the nineteenth century, as Hampton Court ceased to be an official royal residence, the character of the tennis court changed. In 1818 a club committee was established to run what soon became known as 'The Royal Tennis Court'. The Prince of Wales, later Edward VII, learnt to play tennis at Hampton Court and became the club's patron. The club is now the largest in the world with over 750 members (both men and women), although perhaps only a third of this number play regularly. The royal connection is still strong. Queen Elizabeth II is the current patron. In 1980 she attended the celebrations to mark the 450th

Lesley and Chris practising on the court under the initials of William III.

anniversary of the playing of tennis at Hampton Court. Prince Edward is a member of the club and a keen player.

No other court can boast such rich historical and royal associations. 'I can imagine the ghosts out there,' confesses Lesley Ronaldson. 'Henry the Eighth would have played on the land that the court is on, although it was Charles the First who put the first walls around the court that is there today. And all the kings since Victoria's time have been members of the club.'

The duties of the Keeper of the Royal Tennis Court are many and varied. He is responsible for looking after the court, for scoring the matches, coaching the players, training up fellow professionals, stringing the curiously shaped racquets and making the tennis balls. In one respect this marks a recent increase in the keeper's workload: in Tudor times the royal tennis balls were made by the men of the Ironworkers' Company in the City of London.

The actual ball-making process still seems almost medieval – as does the narrow bench-cum-stool that serves as a work surface. Nevertheless, Lesley insists that there has been a steady drift towards modernization. 'The archaeologists found an old ball while digging at the Palace of Westminster,' she says; 'it was made from dog-hair and dog leather. Now we use a core of cork, covered with an old ball-cover, then bound round with cotton webbing and covered with blanket cloth. We get a bolt of the cloth woven up once a year.'

The game has enjoyed something of a revival in recent years with new courts being built in London, Washington and Sydney. Chris Ronaldson has no doubt that London – and Hampton Court – are at the centre of this revival. The staging of the impressive Dresdener Kleinwort Benson Real Tennis Classic at the palace helped to confirm this position. Nick Wood, one of the young professionals at Hampton Court, competed and won the £2,500 singles prize.

Before the tournament, Chris reckoned that despite his relatively limited experience, Nick would have a good chance of winning. 'The fact that he knows the court so well will definitely help him. You see there is no standard size for a real-tennis court. Each one is slightly different. The one here is amongst the biggest. And for a great athlete like Nick that can be an advantage.'

The ever-increasing popularity of the game has produced its own problems – and challenges. 'We are hoping to build a new court here,' says Chris. 'For a long time now we've been the busiest court in the world by some distance; we have a waiting list of almost a hundred people. It's been a ten-year project of ours to get a second court built on the site, not only to improve things for the players but to provide a better facility for people to watch the ancient traditional game that was played here by Cardinal Wolsey and Henry the Eighth. The new court would be designed as much for the spectators as for the players. It would have glass walls and proper seating, and archways for people to watch through.'

It has been a long process gathering all the permissions necessary for such a scheme, but Chris now reckons that they are in a position to put forward an application to Richmond Council. It would be the first new building at Hampton Court for many years but, as Chris points out, 'the palace has always evolved and grown. Bits and pieces have been added on over the centuries. Our own flat here is actually Victorian, although the foundations of the house are Tudor.' The reasons for the popularity of real tennis are many. Chris recalls his

The workshop at the far end of the court is used for racquet-stringing.

own conversion: 'I stumbled across the game really. I had intended to be an ordinary lawn-tennis coach, but I did what I thought was just going to be a winter job at a real-tennis court, and by the time I'd finished the winter I realized this is actually a superior game. And more and more people are finding that out too. As a tactical, technical, physical and mental game, real tennis takes some beating. The cliché is that it is a mixture between lawn tennis, squash and *The Times* crossword. Certainly it's a game where experience counts for a great deal.'

There is always scope for improvement. With so many different court features to play off, it is a game of skill and cunning as much as speed and strength. The club's oldest player is in his eighties and, as Chris points out admiringly, 'he's still actively able to compete and enjoy himself'. Moreover, everyone plays off a handicap so that the level of competition can always be kept up.

While much about the game remains unchanged from the days of Henry VIII and Cardinal Wolsey, there has been some minor updating. 'We now work out everyone's handicap on a computer,' says Lesley. 'It can be adjusted after every match at the push of a button. It's a lot easier than working it all out on paper.'

CLEANING

Over the centuries the cleaning problems at Hampton Court have changed subtly in character and emphasis. When the full court was in residence, it was a constant battle to maintain levels of hygiene and tidiness. Tudor ordinances were frequently concerned with people leaving discarded food about the palace. Today one of the major concerns is dust. It is a constant battle to keep the palace and its collection looking good for the thousands of visitors who pass through.

And, of course, it is these myriad visitors who create the dust. People bring dust in on their clothes, they tread it in on their shoes – particularly during the summer months; and a great deal of dust is just dead skin. Preserving the collection from this steady fall of discarded skin particles is a dedicated team of housekeepers. 'It is easy to start seeing all the visitors as a dust-scattering menace,' explains Helen Smith, the housekeeper responsible for the King's Apartments. 'So it's important for us to remember that we are keeping the palace nice *for* them.'

Although the housekeepers spend much of their time dusting and polishing, they are far removed from the domestic servants of previous centuries. Many of them have university degrees in history of art, archaeology or related subjects; all of them have a keen awareness of the palace's history.

Housekeeper, Helen Smith, tackling a delicate task in the King's Apartments.

Their work, although confined to the collection and the 'areas behind the ropes', is taxing. Some parts of the palace have to be cleaned daily. Delicate pieces are done only once or twice a year. But jobs such as dusting the Grinling Gibbons door-surrounds or polishing the crystal chandelier have to be tackled with extraordinary care and patience.

Although the invention of the vacuum cleaner allows dust to be drawn off, rather than being recirculated in the atmosphere, most of the equipment used by the housekeepers is thoroughly old-fashioned. Elbow grease is still an important commodity. And the housekeepers are all armed with an arsenal of specialist brushes – the softest pony-hair for fragile gilded surfaces, goat's hair for larger areas.

Such specialization and dedication contrast sharply with the days when Georgian housemaids raced around the State Apartments pointing out the pictures to visitors with their feather dusters, and brushing the overmantels as they went.

Dust, however, is not the only enemy. Bugs can be a problem. The Tudor kitchens were recently infested with black-and-white moths. The moth larvae were breeding in the bread rolls displayed there. For authenticity real bread rolls are used, coated in resin to preserve them. The moths, however, had overcome their dislike for the taste of resin and had eaten through it to the bread beyond. The results were not pretty, and there was anxiety that the infestation might migrate to more

Old fabrics require special care and attention.

valuable areas of the palace like tapestries and other soft furnishings.

Caroline Allington, the housekeeper responsible, acted promptly to identify the type of moth and work out a strategy for dealing with it. A specialist 'bug buster' was called in, and the kitchens had to be sprayed with insecticide. Nevertheless as Caroline remarks, 'The insects you can see are usually harmless; it's the ones you can't that are more likely to cause trouble.'

With so much old timber in the palace structure and furniture, both woodworm and deathwatch beetle are major concerns. A degree of caution has to be exercised. As Caroline explains, 'People often get excited over finding old holes in furniture and so on. They don't realize that they are defunct. They can sometimes go as far as using poisons and things on the wood when they don't need to.' To check for woodworm she and her team regularly dry-brush the backs and undersides of the furniture, looking out for the dusty trail of droppings – or 'frass' – that is the sign of recent activity.

Woodworm lay their eggs only in untreated wood, on the unpolished undersides of stools and chairs, or in cracks and crevices. 'The one good thing about them,' concedes Caroline, 'is that the larval stage, which is when the damage occurs, normally takes a minimum of three years to develop.' Regular cleaning of cracks and crevices, and the spaces between floorboards is important in the fight against such bugs. But various new strategies have also been adopted. Heating and cooling wooden artefacts, under carefully controlled conditions, have proved successful methods.

'You can heat something up to above 50 degrees Centigrade,' explains Caroline. 'It may sound a bit drastic, but it's fine. At 50 degrees – for two hours – you'll kill everything: the eggs, the larvae, the pupae and the adult beetles. You just have to make sure the humidity is controlled so that the wood doesn't dry out.' The same effect can be achieved by cooling wood to minus 20 degrees. 'The particularly good thing about the heating method that we are using at the moment,' enthuses Caroline, 'is that it gets rid of any old toxic treatments still lingering in the wood.'

Deathwatch beetle poses a different set of problems. 'The beetles tend to like slightly rotten –

or damp – timbers, particularly oak. As a result they tend to infest massive great structural timbers that have become damp because they are set into walls or roofs and water is penetrating from the outside.'

Attacking the beetles themselves would be a losing battle. 'You need to cure the damp, and that is nearly always a building problem. The damp is getting in because the pointing in the brickwork is bad, or because there is damp rising up from the ground. If you can deal with it, the wood will dry out, the fungus will die, and then the insects will die. That's how we try to manage the problem these days.'

The palace's most famous bug is more picturesque than destructive. The cardinal spider, or *Tegenaria parientina*, has the distinction of being the largest British spider. It is certainly an imposing arachnid, often up to five inches across, with a plump reddish-brown body and long jointed hairy legs.

Its exact connection with Hampton Court and especially Cardinal Wolsey, although universally acknowledged, is somewhat undefined. Some have suggested a historical encounter between Wolsey and the spider, others have hinted at a symbolic association between the web-spinning spider and the policy-spinning Wolsey. Caroline Allington suggests a more prosaic link: 'They are called cardinal spiders because they appear to have a large cross on their backs.'

It is often stated that the spider is found only at Hampton Court. This, however, is not quite correct. The *Collins Field Guide* to spiders indicates that the cardinal spider is to be found only in 'very old houses' in the southeastern counties of England, while another guide mentions that the spider is 'particular about her address and only stays in the best localities'. Nevertheless, given these various constraints, it is easy to understand why the palace should have become a favoured place of habitation for *Tegenaria parientina*; there are few buildings older than Hampton Court in the southeastern counties, and none grander.

Although the housekeeping team tries to keep cobwebs out of the palace rooms, the spider finds congenial habitats elsewhere. Cardinal spiders can often be seen in the arches above the doorways in Fountain Court. Given their enthusiasm for eating smaller bugs, the spiders must be accounted useful additions to the housekeeping team, rather than pests.

Jill Taylor and Caroline Allington in the palace kitchens.

CHAPTER 5

A NEW VERSAILLES

*I*n February 1689, soon after acceding to the throne, William and Mary visited Hampton Court. The place appealed to them at once. The flatness of the park, together with Charles II's lime-flanked canal, was reminiscent of Holland. There was the attraction, too, of good hunting, and the convenience of proximity to London. It seems that even on this first visit the royal couple conceived the idea of making the palace their principal residence.

They returned the following month for a longer stay. The Queen, according to the Duchess of Marlborough, examined everything, 'looking into every closet and conveniency, and turning up the quilts upon the beds, as people do when they come into an inn, and with no other sort of concern in her appearance but such as they express'.

OPPOSITE The grand approach to the King's Apartments, decorated by Antonio Verrio. ABOVE William and Mary's initials.

Mary's verdict after this grand tour of inspection was not entirely favourable. She considered that changes would have to be made. The old Tudor buildings were deemed outmoded. She and William thought that they needed a modern and impressive setting for their rule. They consulted the Surveyor General, Sir Christopher Wren, and asked him to rebuild the palace for them.

Wren relished the prospect. He was aware of the new court architecture that had evolved in France. Louis XIV's palaces at the Louvre and Versailles were recognized as the acme of European royal chic. Wren wanted a chance to match their high Renaissance elegance. He proposed a 'Grand Design' for Hampton Court. It would involve demolishing almost the entire Tudor palace and realigning the site. Only Henry VIII's Great Hall was to be retained, as the centrepiece of a new line of approach from the north. The surviving drawings indicate the grandeur and originality of Wren's conception.

Sir Godfrey Kneller's portraits of William III and Mary II, who started their reign as joint monarchs.

It was, perhaps, too grand. Time and money were limited. It was decided to modify the scheme, and to make an immediate start only upon a new set of Royal Apartments. Although Wren's vision for this building was new, the template on which he worked was already established. He preserved the existing Tudor layout of two sets of royal apartments running around the Cloister Green Court, the King's on the south side, facing out over the Privy Garden, the Queen's State Apartments on the east front, looking down the imposing vista established by Charles II. Internally, the time-honoured royal form was preserved: the succession of rooms, each leading on from the other in a hierarchical progress towards the royal inner sanctum. Although Wren was concerned to dress this conventional arrangement in a new style, he decided to echo something of the palace's existing character by using brick as his primary material. To give the building a greater elegance, however, all the major features were to be picked out in Portland stone.

To provide a fitting entrance to the State Rooms from the Tudor muddle of Clock Court, Wren designed a gracious colonnade, running along the south side of the courtyard. Visitors would pass through it to reach the grand stairway up to the King's Apartments.

Work on the apartments began in May 1689. It proceeded apace. William wanted quick results. The old Tudor buildings around Cloister Green Court were speedily demolished, as were the Duchess of Cleveland's lodgings. New buildings began to rise in their place. The King and Queen had intended to make Windsor their country retreat for the duration of the building work but an outbreak of smallpox in the town persuaded them to move to the building site at Hampton Court.

The King was much criticized for spending so much of his time away from London, and so much of his revenue on an expensive new building project. He would go up to town, 'only on Council days' and sometimes not even then. One of his ministers, Lord Halifax, complained that often the Council met out at Hampton Court and the Council members 'every time they went to see him, lost five hours in going and coming'.

He was away in London, however, towards the end of the year, when a large section of the new south range collapsed. Two workmen were killed and eleven others were injured. An inquiry was launched. Wren was instructed to prepare a report on the accident, and ordered to exercise 'some haste, for the King is of the opinion ye building is in a bad condition'. Wren found himself in dispute with William Talman, the ambitious Comptroller of Works, who doubted the quality of the work being done. The Treasury appointed independent arbitrators to inspect it. They exonerated Wren, suggesting that the cause of the disaster lay in the haste with which the building work was going forward. Work resumed at a more measured pace.

King William was often out of England during the early years of the reign. He spent much time in Ireland, quelling the supporters of James II, and even more in his native Holland, supervising an Anglo–Dutch action against the French. During his absences Queen Mary spent her time at Hampton Court. In an attempt to escape the noise and dust of the building work she moved into the rooms in the Water Gallery that were previously used by Lady Castlemaine. The apartment was repaired and redecorated for her use under Wren's direction. Elegant door-surrounds and cornices were set up, carved with festoons of fruit and flowers by Grinling Gibbons; the ceilings were painted with allegorical designs and specially tiered fireplaces were fitted, on which Queen Mary might display her collections of Oriental and blue-and-white china. There was a Looking-Glass Closet, decorated with mirrors and mural paintings, a Delft-Ware Closet for the pride of the Queen's collection, and a richly finished Marble Closet. For comfort and convenience a modern Bathing Closet was also installed. Daniel Defoe was much impressed with this last room, describing it as 'very fine, suited either to hot or cold bathing, as the season should invite'. Jean Tijou, the great French ironmaster, and one of the many exceptional designers brought to work at Hampton Court, was commissioned to refashion the little iron balcony looking out over the river. Below the balcony a small private garden was laid out for the Queen on the tiny quadrant of ground between the Mount Garden and the riverbank. The little dairy was preserved and provided the Queen with a quaint diversion.

Queen Mary took a close interest in the work advancing on the new apartments. As Wren recorded, she 'pleased herself from time to time in examining and surveying the drawings,

contrivances and the whole progress of the present building and in giving thereon her own judgement, which was exquisite; and there were few arts or sciences in which her Majesty had not only an elegant taste but a knowledge much superior to any of her sex in that, or it may be any former, age'.

She kept the King, away on his campaigns, informed of progress. Indeed there was sometimes a connection between the two spheres of war and architecture. At one point work slowed down on site due to the lack of Portland stone for the dressings of the façade. As the Queen explained to her husband, 'the French are in the Channel and at Present between Portland and us, from whence the stone must come'. As a compromise Wren was obliged to use Bath stone instead for the inner east range of his new courtyard. The substitution pleased neither the architect nor the Queen. The stone was softer and more prone to weathering. Two centuries later it had to be replaced with Portland stone.

Happily, sufficient supplies of Portland stone were already on site to adorn the rest of the building. The two great outward-facing ranges soon took shape. Each was built on three storeys with a double-height first floor which housed the State Apartments. The east-facing façade was dominated by a central section of four Corinthian half columns and four Corinthian pilasters, supporting a cornice and a decorated pediment, carved by Caius Cibber, showing Hercules overcoming Envy. The image was just one of several Herculean references introduced into the building's decoration. King William felt that he had a particular affinity with the Greek hero.

The central portion of Wren's East Front, with its pediment by Caius Cibber.

Sir Christopher Wren oversaw the transformation of Hampton Court.

The southern front is slightly more restrained. The stone-clad central feature is narrower than its counterpart on the eastern façade, the sculptural flourishes less profuse. The entwined royal arms of William and Mary do, however, surmount two of the flanking windows on the *piano nobile*. The drainpipe-heads carry the date 1690, suggesting something of the speed with which the work was carried forward. In Wren's original design four lead statues stood on the parapet of the central section.

The inward-looking façades of the new ranges made up two sides of an internal courtyard. This new courtyard replaced the former Cloister Green Court. It maintained – in a new style – the form of a cloister, with an arched arcade running around it at ground level. In the middle of the space Wren set a fountain in a large, simple circular pond. The Herculean motif of the east-front pediment was carried through in the carved lion-skin wreaths surrounding the circular windows of the first-floor half-storey. It was stated even more forcefully in the twelve painted panels depicting the Labours of Hercules which decorated the blank window-spaces on the south side of the courtyard; these were the work of Louis Laguerre, an accomplished French artist and the son-in-law of Jean Tijou.

Wren and his royal patrons had conceived their design as an integrated scheme involving both the palace and its grounds. The King and Queen were keen gardeners. It was said of William that 'in the least interval of Ease, Gard'ning took up a great part of his Time, in which he was not only a great Delighter but likewise a great Judge'. Together with

Mary he had already established important gardens in Holland at Honselaardsijk and Het Loo. They had been helped in their work by the Dutch architect Daniel Marot, and by William's great favourite, Willem Bentinck. Bentinck accompanied the King to England and was made both Earl of Portland and Superintendent of the Royal Gardens. The management of the Royal Gardens was put on a new, more organized footing. Bentinck's deputy was George London, the leading designer of gardens for the English nobility; and their Comptroller of Works was the ubiquitous Talman.

In tandem with the development of the new Royal Apartments, plans were drawn up to modify the gardens and grounds of the palace. Although the

*Looking down on the Lower Orangery
and its garden*

*A magnificent panorama of Hampton Court painted
by Leonard Knyff, c.1703*

grand scheme of realigning (and rebuilding) the whole palace had been put on hold, a great Chestnut Avenue was planted along the proposed northern approach through Bushy Park, in case the scheme should be taken up again later. Charles II's grand eastward vista was remodelled. His canal was shortened at the palace end, to allow the semicircular plot in front of the Queen's Apartments to be increased in size and replanted, according to designs by Marot. It was transformed into the Great Fountain Garden. One giant fountain was set up in the middle of the space, surrounded by twelve smaller fountains, all playing in unison. At least that was the theory. The system never worked very well, and there are frequent entries in the accounts for repairs and improvements.

The ground was divided up into a series of grand parterres. There were areas of *parterre de broderie*, scrolling lacework patterns of low box hedging set in gravel, and sections of *gazon coup*, turf cut into motifs surrounded by coloured sand or crushed brick. Around the border of each of these great parterres stood – at intervals – yew trees and white holly-bushes trimmed into the shape of obelisks. Along the western edge of the garden were set twelve magnificent panels of ornate *repoussé* work, the masterpieces of Jean Tijou.

Queen Mary certainly involved herself closely in the development of the gardens, but her particular horticultural interest was more specialized. She collected 'exoticks'. She had already established an impressive collection of rare plants in Holland. Many of her best specimens were, in due course, shipped over to Hampton Court. She had gathered species from around the globe, sponsoring plant collectors on trips to such places as Virginia, Barbados, the Canary Islands and the Cape of Good Hope. Amongst her prized rarities were several examples of the *Agave americana variegata*, which was reputed to take a hundred years to flower. The care of her collections was entrusted to her personal botanist, Dr Leonard Plukenet, who received a handsome stipend of £2,000.

It was he, perhaps, who oversaw the constantly manured 'hot beds', laid out just north of the kitchen range, where exotic seeds could be germinated. He was certainly involved in the construction of three large 'glass cases', or greenhouses, along the northern side of Henry VIII's old Pond Gardens, on the site of what is now the Lower Orangery. Each of these structures was equipped with four stoves to provide a constant warmth during the winter months. The Queen also ordered the draining of the three rectangular fishponds. One of them was used to grow flowers for use in the State Apartments, but the other two provided sheltered gardens, where citrus trees and auriculas could be placed outside during the summer months. The central section of the ground floor in the new south range, facing on to the Privy Garden, was also designed as an Orangery. It provided additional winter shelter for the army of potted orange trees that William and Mary had shipped over from Holland as living symbols of the House of Orange.

Work on the Privy Garden itself had to wait until the major construction work on the palace was finished. The garden was used as the main works yard for the palace builders. It was, throughout the early years of the new reign, filled with materials. A scattering of wooden site huts had also been erected for Wren, London and others. By 1690, however, a start could be made. A raised terrace was built along the eastern edge of the garden to match the one already existing on the other side. A new trellised bower was planted on the eastern terrace, running almost the whole length of the garden. All Henry VIII's buildings were removed: the gallery and towers along the east wall, the gazebo on top of the Mount, and the Mount itself. For the time being the length of the garden was not extended down to the river. The wreckage of the old Mount garden was discreetly hidden behind a trellis screen pending further funds.

The garden was laid out in a simple quartered plan with cut-work – or *gazon coup* – designs of grass and gravel in the four plots. The grand fountain of Arethusa was equipped with a new basin of Portland stone and moved to a central position towards the bottom end of the garden.

Even though this arrangement marked only the first step of a more ambitious scheme, it pleased the Queen at once. The new bower on the west terrace became a favourite haunt for her and her ladies-in-waiting. They would pass their time under its shade with needlework and gossip.

In a conscious attempt to echo the merry distinction of Charles II's court, the Queen commissioned her Principal Painter, Sir Godfrey Kneller, to paint *The Hampton Court Beauties*, a second series of portraits of the ladies 'attending her majesty'. Although Lady Dorchester advised against the project on the grounds that it would provoke the jealousy of those not asked to sit, the series seems to have been popular. It was much admired by Defoe. The Queen hung the portraits in her own apartment in the Water Gallery.

The happy court life created by the Queen ended abruptly in 1694 with her death from smallpox. She died at Kensington Palace. She had never had the chance to inhabit her new apartments at Hampton Court. After five years' work and an expenditure of some £113,000 (about £8 million at today's prices) the structure was complete but the decoration was, as yet, unstarted.

WORK COMPLETED

The Queen's death brought all work at the palace to a halt. King William seems to have been genuinely distraught at the loss of his wife. And his grief, quite as much as his commitments out of England and the limitations of his budget, seems to have occasioned the break in activity. The hiatus lasted three years.

By 1697 the period of mourning was over. Moreover the peace of Rijswijk in that year freed William from his military concerns. He had more time and more money and he turned his attention once again to Hampton Court. His attention became even more focused early in the following year when the royal palace at Whitehall burnt down. William asked both Wren and Talman to prepare estimates for the completion of the interiors of the King's Apartments at Hampton Court. Wren's estimate – based on the original schemes he had drawn up almost ten years beforehand – came to £6,800; Talman proposed a new and simpler scheme for £5,500, and his tender was accepted. Wren, well into his sixties and heavily occupied with his work at St Paul's, does not seem to have minded being undercut by his younger rival.

Work proceeded through the summer of 1699 while the King was abroad. He returned from Holland in October and pronounced himself 'extremely well-pleased' with the decoration going forward. By the end of the month he was even able to spend his first night in the new apartments. Such were his excitement and impatience to see the scheme completed, he altered his plan of lodging at Windsor Castle. Instead he flitted between London and Hampton Court. He devoted his time to supervising the decoration of the apartments and the layout of the gardens. The records reveal the extent to which he involved himself in the details of the job. Fireplaces were moved, pictures rehung, and rooms altered. And this process continued even after April 1700 when the King took up formal residence with his court for the first time. Indeed during the two remaining years of his reign he was constantly refining the layout and decoration of the palace and its grounds. At the end of each of his sojourns he would leave a list of instructions for further improvements. No detail was too trivial. The white curtains in his closet were, within months of being installed, changed for red ones.

The decorative work carried out under William's supervision combined a certain formality of effect with passages of rather bold baroque ornamentation. He was fortunate in the craftsmen available to him. Grinling Gibbons, then at the height of his powers, supplied many of the carved limewood overmantels and picture surrounds, wonderfully fluent swags of fruit, foliage and flowers. Jean Tijou, who had established a workshop on Hampton Court Green just outside the palace gates, contributed the elegant, scrolled iron balustrade to the grand staircase by which the King's Apartments were reached. The beautifully crafted – and ornately chased – locks on the doors were the work of the aptly named Josiah Key (whom Talman described as 'the most ingenious man in Europe').

Responsibility for the movable furnishings in the Apartments fell to the King's Master of the

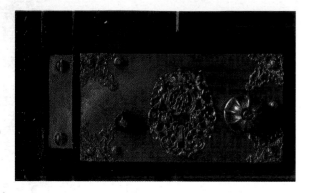

ABOVE *One of the locks made for the King's Apartments by Josiah Key.* RIGHT *The East Front viewed from across the Fountain Garden.*

Wardrobe, Ralph, First Earl of Montagu. He was a man of both taste and knowledge, He had spent much time in France as an ambassador to the court of Louis XIV. He sought work from many of the finest craftsmen of the day. He commissioned numerous cabinets, firebacks, pier tables, chairs of estate and chandeliers. The richest textiles were used to provide the swagged, fringed and tasselled drapes for curtains, canopies and bed-hangings. He ordered pier glasses from Gerrit Jensen, torchères and tables by Jean Pelletier, and silver sconces by Philip Rollos. Much of the beautiful walnut 'seat furniture' was made by Thomas Roberts, who held the King's warrant as Joiner to the Royal Household.

Everything was pressed into service to make an effect. Following a recently established fashion, the King commissioned his gunsmith, John Harris, to arrange a magnificent display of arms on the upper walls of the Guard Chamber. Some 3,000 pieces – halberds, swords, muskets, pistols, bayonets, drums – were ranged in intricate patterns and motifs, providing an ingenious suggestion of military might as well as an attractive piece of decoration. Grinling Gibbons, or his workshop,

The King's Little Bedchamber, its overmantle decked with fine porcelain.

Charles II, who employed him on the decoration of Windsor Castle. He also did work at Chatsworth, Burghley and other important English houses. It was a feature of his work to include sly portraits of friends and enemies in the allegorical scenes which he depicted. For the Grand Staircase he took as his theme a fourth-century satire, written by the Roman Emperor Julian the Apostate. Julian's poem told of Alexander the Great's triumph over the Caesars; in Verrio's version William was represented as Alexander, triumphing over his Stuart forebears. The artist also managed to insinuate into the composition the obligatory reference to William's titular deity, Hercules. The Greek hero duly appears as an intermediary, introducing Alexander to the gods. And on a less exalted level it is thought he used the features of Anne Marriott, the buxom daughter of King William's 'Keeper of the Standing Wardrobe', for Atropos, the Fate who cuts the Thread of Life. She is supposed to have spurned his amorous advances.

Abandoning the prevailing severity of the outer rooms, Verrio was also employed to decorate the ceilings of William's Great and Little Bedchambers. The former he enriched with a vision of Endymion in the arms of Morpheus, the Greek god of Sleep; the latter with one of Mars, the god of War, lolling in the lap of Venus.

A less intimate symbolism was adopted for the picture-hanging in the outer State Rooms. Portraits abounded of William's Stuart ancestors and connections, reinforcing the message of his royal heritage and of his legitimate rule. To set the tone, a vast canvas entitled *William III on Horseback*, by Kneller, greeted visitors to the Presence Chamber.

The State Bed in the Great Bedchamber.

supplied fine carved wooden 'targets' as centrepieces for the displays. A beautiful oval plaque, carved with the monogram of William and Mary, was fixed above the fireplace, at the centre of an arrangement of sword blades and pistols, 'sett like the starr in the Garter'. Although some of the arms in the room – as it now stands – date from the mid-eighteenth century, the general arrangement of them is very close to what William and his courtiers would have known.

More conventional forms of art also lent their weight to the imposing magnificence of William's scheme. The walls of the Grand Staircase were painted by the Italian-born court painter, Antonio Verrio. Verrio had been invited to England by

Family portraits were not, however, the only masterworks that the King rescued from the obscurity of the royal collection. One of his first acts on taking control of the palace decoration was to order the framing and hanging of the great series of Raphael's cartoons, acquired by Charles I but never before displayed. He wanted them to decorate the length of the gallery, which ran along the inside line of the King's Apartments. The arrangement necessitated closing off the door between the gallery and the Privy Chamber. The drawings were intended – initially – for the King's private pleasure. With the closing-off of the doorway through into the Privy Chamber, the only access to the gallery was via a little door in the King's Bedchamber. But when the court began to reside at Hampton Court for extended periods, and the Privy Council was obliged to meet there, William soon discovered that the gallery was the only room suitable for their meetings. New arrangements had to be made. He promptly had the empty Queen's Gallery set up as his own private space, hanging it with Mantegna's *Triumphs of Caesar* after they had been restored by Louis Laguerre.

King William also made good use of the unrivalled collection of tapestries assembled by Henry VIII and added to by subsequent monarchs. He had choice sets repaired and cleaned ready for use. He was delighted to find one tapestry depicting the Triumph of Hercules. He hung it in the Presence Chamber.

The layout of the State Apartments offered little scope for innovation. The order of the enfilade of great rooms – Guard Chamber, Presence Chamber, Eating Room (where the King occasionally dined before the court), Privy Chamber, Withdrawing Room and Great Bedchamber – was fixed by long tradition and current court practice. And their furnishing was similarly limited by custom. As courtiers were not allowed to sit in the King's presence, furniture was largely superfluous. A single chair of estate on a low dais, set beneath a rich canopy, sufficed for the furnishing of the Presence Chamber.

Beyond the State Rooms proper lay the King's private apartments, under the charge of the Groom of the Stool, the Earl of Portland. These rooms included, at the far end of the first floor, the Little Bedchamber, with its 'stool room', and a study where William could work. Below them, connected by a private stair, were a private dining-room, drawing-room, bedroom and music room.

Although he had devoted so much energy to creating a magnificent set of State Apartments, the King preferred to pass his time in these private rooms. In part this seems to have been a matter of temperament. The historian Macaulay describes William's lack of social grace.

He was in truth far better qualified to save a nation than to adorn a court... He seldom came forth from his closet, and when he appeared in the public rooms, he stood among the crowd of courtiers and ladies, stern and abstracted, making no jest, and smiling at none. His freezing look, his silence, the dry and concise answers which he uttered when he could keep silence no longer, disgusted noblemen and gentlemen who had been accustomed to be slapped on the back by their royal masters... He spoke our language, but not well. His accent was foreign: his diction was inelegant; and his vocabulary seems to have been no larger than was necessary for the transaction of business.

Away from the expectations of courtly intercourse he fared better. In his private rooms, amongst his intimates, the King could allow protocol to be relaxed a little. His great favourite during the latter part of his reign was Arnold Joost van Keppel, a young Dutch retainer, whom he made Earl of Albemarle and a Knight of the Garter to the manifest disgust of the English lords. When the King was away from Hampton Court, the ground-floor suite was made available to the Earl of Albemarle (as a supplement to the apartment he already had on the second floor).

The King's private rooms – or closets – were furnished in an intimate and domestic style. They were decorated with some of the smaller treasures of the royal collection – Jacopo Bassano's *Portrait of a Man Holding Gloves*, Van Dyck's oil-sketch for *Charles I on Horseback*, and the same artist's portrait of *Margaret Lemon*. All the pictures were hung from rails on silken cords to allow for easy rearrangement. In the private dining-room at the west end of the Orangery, William set up Kneller's *Hampton Court Beauties*, removed from the Queen's old rooms in the Water Gallery.

The quaint old Water Gallery itself was demolished as part of William's scheme to extend the Privy Garden down to the river. The whole level of the garden had to be lowered and set on a slope to provide a clear view of the water from the Orangery terrace. A new parterre was laid out. And Tijou's magnificent screen, which had been removed from the Great Fountain Garden on the east front, was set up at the far end of the garden.

The Tijou Screen in their current position at the end of the Privy Garden.

To compensate for the loss of the Water Gallery, William commissioned Wren to design a small crenellated Banqueting House close to the river, beyond the walls of the Glass Case Garden. Some of the fabric and decoration from the Water Gallery was reused in the new building. The wonderfully ornate interior was carved by Gibbons and painted by Verrio, to provide a perfect setting for intimate suppers.

William's plans for the Hampton Court gardens were not confined to the south front. He revived his idea of establishing an impressive northern approach through Bushy Park. A grandiose causeway was constructed down the Chestnut Avenue. The statue of Arethusa – now mistakenly taken for Diana – was moved from the Privy Garden to a site half way down the avenue. It was set in a gigantic circular pond surrounded by a circle of trees.

Henry VIII's Tilt Yard was also remodelled. William demolished all but one of the viewing-towers and divided up the space into six walled kitchen gardens.

The gateways to the palace were embellished. At the main, western entrance, William set up the Trophy Gates to commemorate his military victories, with their two outer piers surmounted by

The Banqueting House created by William III as a place of recreation.

The Lion and the Unicorn on the Trophy Gates stand sentinel outside the palace.

arms, and their two inner piers topped with a lion and a unicorn cast in 'Hard Metall' by the master-mason, John Oliver. These majestic guardians still greet the visitor to the palace. At the northern end of the Broadwalk William erected the Flower-Pot Gates, two Portland stone piers, carved with his initials and royal insignia. At the other end of the Broadwalk he laid out a new pathway, running along the riverbank to a new bowling green. The green itself he surrounded with four trim little pavilions designed by Wren. Only one of these survives, converted into a private residence.

Nor was this all. In the garden plot directly to the north of the palace, George London and his assistant, Henry Wise, created the inaptly named Wilderness: a formal garden of clipped box hedges. It included, near its centre, a flat, circular 'Troy Town maze', cut in the turf, to provide a variation from the straight lines of the other walks. Defoe

considered the arrangement delightful: 'Nothing of that kind,' he wrote, 'can be more beautiful.' Others were less impressed. One critic complained of the 'regular straight walks', adding that 'one might faint for shade on a sultry day' in such a garden.

William had barely begun to enjoy the splendid setting he had created when he made his fatal hunting expedition in the park in February 1702. He was suffering badly from dropsy and, in spite of medical opinion, insisted that riding was the best way of easing the pain in his legs. 'While I endeavoured to make the horse change his walking into a gallop,' he recalled on his deathbed, 'he fell upon his knees. Upon that I meant to raise him with the bridle, but he fell on one side, and so I fell with my right shoulder upon the ground. 'Tis a strange thing for it happened upon a smooth level ground.' The horse, it seems, had stumbled on a molehill. The King's collarbone was broken. Complications ensued and he died two weeks later at Kensington Palace.

THE SMELL OF BOX

*The Privy Garden, on the south side
of the palace, has been restored to its form under
William III.*

William was succeeded by Queen Anne, the younger sister of his wife, Mary. She was thirty-seven when she came to the throne, plain, plump and married to the amiable, but greedy, Prince George of Denmark. It was Defoe who first suggested that Hampton Court was loved only by alternate monarchs. And certainly his observation held good in this case. Anne had little affection for her deceased brother-in-law (who, amongst many acts of calculated discourtesy, had once failed to offer her a dish of garden peas). She was not anxious to complete his expensive building schemes. She preferred to use Windsor Castle as her main country retreat.

Nevertheless Hampton Court was easily accessible from Windsor and she did make brief forays to the palace and its park. Alexander Pope memorably enshrined the association in the lines:

Close by those meads, for ever crown'd with flow'rs,
Where Thames with pride surveys his rising Tow'rs
There stands a structure of majestic frame,
Which from the neighb'ring Hampton takes
   its name.
Here Britain's statesmen oft the fall foredoom
Of foreign Tyrants, and of Nymphs at home;
Here Thou, great Anna! Whom three realms obey,
Dost sometimes counsel take – and sometimes Tea.

What he achieved at Hampton Court has, however, lived on. The recent restoration of the King's Apartments has returned those rooms back to the grandeur and glory of his original vision. And the Privy Garden too has been brought back into harmony with the building before which it stands.

Throughout Anne's reign the Privy Council continued to hold more than occasional meetings in the Cartoon Gallery. She also received several diplomatic missions at the palace, including one, in 1713, from the 'Envoy Extraordinary of the Czar of Muscovy'.

The Queen did not neglect the palace completely, or its grounds. She made several minor alterations to the gardens. It was Queen Anne who ordered the planting of the maze, which still stands to the north of the palace, in what was the Wilderness. Near to it she also set up two piers for a gateway that she left unfinished. And she replaced Queen Mary's three glass cases with what is now called the Lower Orangery.

More importantly, Queen Anne remodelled the Great Fountain Garden. She got Henry Wise to dig the semicircular canal around its edge. And she simplified the design of the parterre considerably, replacing the low scrolling hedges with areas of plain lawn. It has been suggested that she was motivated in this by her dislike of the smell of box, but both economy and taste probably played their part in her decision. The upkeep of an elaborate *parterre de broderie* was considerable, and the new arrangement seems also to have been more in keeping with Wren's original conception for the gardens. Certainly the new layout was considered to be in 'The English Style'.

In the park the Queen commissioned Wise to lay out a network of curving drives, or 'chaise

The famous Hampton Court maze was one of Queen Anne's few additions to the gardens.

Queen Anne, by the fashionable court painter,
Godfrey Kneller.

expenditure. Throughout her reign she was petitioned by craftsmen who had undertaken work for her predecessor and had not been paid.

Within the palace Anne effected few changes. When in residence she lodged in the King's Apartments. She did, however, make one move to complete the still-unfinished Queen's Apartments on the East Front. She commissioned the ageing Verrio to decorate the Queen's Drawing Room with a richly detailed 'Allegory of British Naval Power'. The Queen herself appears in idealized form on one wall receiving the homage of four continents; her husband is also depicted, in his official role as Lord Admiral, the fleet behind him. Upon the ceiling the Queen is shown again, as Justice, surrounded by the attendant personifications of Peace, Plenty and Britannia. Shortly after finishing the work Verrio's eyesight failed. The Queen provided him with a pension and allowed him to live on at Hampton Court. He died there in 1707 and was buried in the local church.

Verrio was not the only servant of the palace whom Anne honoured. The Queen also granted Sir Christopher Wren the lease on a house on Hampton Court Green, so that he might have a base close to his great creation. Although well into his seventies, Wren continued in his post as Surveyor General and took a close interest in any work carried out at Hampton Court.

Anne also remodelled the Chapel. The magnificent Tudor ceiling was preserved but other original features were swept away. At the east end, behind the altar, she set up the beautiful reredos, designed by Wren and carved by Gibbons. The screen had originally been intended for Whitehall but had barely been begun when that palace was burnt down in 1698. It was subsequently modified and finished for Hampton Court, and erected in

ridings', so that she could hunt 'with more ease and safety in her chaise or coach'. Her gout made riding quite uncomfortable. Jonathan Swift set down a description of the Queen in his *Journal to Stella*: 'she hunts in a chaise with one horse, which she drives herself, and drives furiously like Jehu and is a mighty hunter like Nimrod'.

The laying out of the drives proved more expensive than Wise had estimated. When Anne complained of the fact, her gardener explained that 'a great hill in Kingston Avenue, which obstructed the view from the House and Gardens' had needed to be levelled. The grand scale of Wise's vision and the Queen's concern for economy were both typical. After the extravagance of King William's schemes, Anne seems to have exercised a close control on

1708. She also installed a new organ, which – modified by the latest in electronic technology – is still used for services in the Chapel.

To increase the light the old Tudor windows were removed and larger, casement windows were put in. On the south wall – where the window no longer gave on to a courtyard – a *trompe l'oeil* window was painted giving a 'view' of Fountain Court. The work was done by James Thornhill, who was emerging as the successor to Verrio's crown. Thornhill also painted both the Queen's monogram and motto (*Semper Eadem*: Always the Same) on the walls between the windows, and decorated the ceiling of the Royal Pew. The Royal Pew itself was remodelled. Instead of being divided into two equal sections, one for the King and the other for the Queen, Anne arranged it with a central chamber, with her throne set in the middle.

Her position had become sadly solitary. Her husband died in 1708, and their only child, William, Duke of Gloucester, had died some years before, aged only eleven. In order to exclude the Catholic descendants of James II from the succession, an Act of Settlement was arranged. The crown was to pass to the Protestant branch of the family, the descendants of Charles I's sister, Elizabeth, who had married Frederick V, Elector Palatine of the Rhine.

The greatest drama played out at Hampton Court during Queen Anne's reign was not a royal one but a wonderfully absurd scandal involving a group of fashionable courtiers. The details of how Lord Petrie provoked the wrath of Miss Arabella Fermor, by surreptitiously snipping off a lock of her hair during a card party at the palace, were blown up by Alexander Pope into his mock-epic

The interior of the Chapel Royal was remodelled and refurbished by Queen Anne.

masterpiece, 'The Rape of the Lock'. The wit of the poem, it is said, helped to reconcile the feuding parties. It also enshrines an enduring image of the pleasures of courtly life at Hampton Court during the first years of the eighteenth century.

> *Hither the heroes and the nymphs resort,*
> *To taste awhile the pleasures of a Court;*
> *In various talk th' instructive hours they passed*
> *Who gave the ball, or paid the visit last;*
> *One speaks the glory of the British Queen,*
> *And one describes a charming Indian screen;*
> *A third interprets motions, looks and eyes;*
> *At ev'ry word a reputation dies.*
> *Snuff, or the fan, supply each pause of chat,*
> *With singing, laughing, ogling, and all that.*

GARDENS

'*T*he great thing about Hampton Court,' says Terry Gough, 'is that the gardens have always developed together with the palace. They are all part of the same thing.' Terry Gough is the current Head Gardener at Hampton Court. He is clearly alive to the great traditions of his job: above his desk hang the portraits of two of his illustrious predecessors – Henry Wise and Lancelot 'Capability' Brown.

Modern times, however, have brought new challenges and new methods. 'Our work, over the year, is divided between maintenance and special project work.' The busiest times in the garden are between March and the end of October. During this period the members of the gardening staff are kept busy with a constant succession of tasks. Besides the 750 acres of parkland around the palace, there are 60 acres of formal garden which, as Terry says, 'all require intensive horticultural maintenance'.

The figures are formidable. The formal flowerbeds are all planted twice a year: the spring flowers are put in in October, the summer bedding at the end of spring. Over 140,000 bedding plants are grown on site in the nursery at the palace, many raised from cuttings. And a whole separate double-rotation cycle of planting is carried out in the Privy Garden, using historically accurate plants which, as Terry explains, are both 'more expensive and

Traditional gardening methods are often the best.

more delicate'. Meanwhile in the Wilderness section of the garden – which has developed into an informal wild garden – over 200,000 spring bulbs are planted each year.

'Planting out is very time-consuming,' says Terry. 'But as with many garden tasks there is no short cut. It's the same with weeding. We don't use chemical weedkillers here, except on some of the paths, so everything has to be done by hand.' The most labour-intensive task is, apparently, topiary. 'We've been experimenting with a new hoist to help us cut the large yews on the East Front, but it's still a very time-consuming job.'

Some areas, however, have proved more susceptible to technological innovation. 'We are always looking for ways to improve our efficiency,' insists Terry. 'We go to the machinery show at Windsor each year to assess what is available. We used to use 36-inch pedestrian mowing machines for cutting the lawns because we needed to get a very fine cut. Now we have been able to switch to the little tractors used for cutting golf greens. They are able to provide a result of a sufficiently high standard.'

All the garden work is now planned and scheduled on computer. 'We are able to provide the staff with monthly work sheets with specifications – and even safety information – relating to each job.' Planting programmes are also worked out on computer. And recently a database of all the trees on the estate has been completed.

The selective use of technology has greatly increased the efficiency of the garden work. In the days of Henry Wise the garden staff numbered hundreds. When Terry first came to Hampton Court there were over eighty gardeners. Now the work is done by forty-one people.

It is very much a team operation. Everyone is encouraged to suggest ideas and to make observations. Within this scheme the day-to-day running of the gardens falls largely to the Deputy Gardens and Estate Manager, Graham Dillamore, and his assistant Gary Wise. The two of them have a regular 'Tuesday morning walk around' to check on the state of work – and to argue over planting plans, colour schemes and other matters.

They both recognize the peculiar challenge of the Hampton Court gardens. 'It's a bit of a balancing act,' admits Graham, 'trying to maintain the historical integrity of the gardens, which is really important. But at the same time, we've got visitors who enjoy flowers and enjoy beautiful-looking gardens, and we've got to make sure the gardens look attractive. And I think we do manage to achieve that balance.'

During the winter recess, when the pace of maintenance work slows down, Terry and his colleagues have a chance to turn their attention to the special projects adumbrated in their ten-year garden strategy. In recent years these have included the magnificent reconstruction of William III's Privy Garden in all its early-eighteenth-century formality and splendour.

To provide a framework for such schemes the grounds and gardens are divided into about a dozen 'character areas', such as the Wilderness, the Tilt Yard, the East Front, the Barge Walk, the Pond Gardens, and the Privy Garden. Each one has a distinctive flavour which Terry and his team seek to enhance.

Mowing the lawn the old-fashioned way in the Lower Orangery garden.

'One of the areas we are looking at at the moment,' says Terry, 'is the West Front and the Barge Walk, as these are the first things most people see as they walk over Hampton Court Bridge from the station. We are considering ways to improve the layout: changing the path surfaces, extending the areas of grass and perhaps breaking up the line of trees to give a better view of the palace from the bridge. There is also a suggestion that we might timber-clad some of the concrete buildings down by the waterfront in order to improve the general character of the scene.'

His own particular project is centred on Queen Mary II's long-dispersed collection of 'exoticks'. During a sabbatical year at the Architectural Association he produced a dissertation on the subject, searching out the original plant lists, tracing contemporary container designs, and discovering – from the study of old prints – how they were displayed. The Queen, using her international contacts – not least with the Dutch East India Company – gathered together one of the great collections of rare plants, including many choice agaves, aloes and citrus trees. And she displayed them at Hampton Court in a manner calculated to impress: each specimen was set in its own specially decorated container.

There are now plans to re-create a collection of typical exotics from that period for public display in a historically accurate manner. 'It is a gradual thing that we will be working on over the next five or six years,' says Terry. 'We will have to grow a lot of the plants specially. We have asked Kew Gardens to help with providing propagation material.' There are very few surviving plant pots from the period, but Terry has traced many of the elaborate designs, especially from the Netherlands, and plans to re-create them.

Terry Gough, the Head Gardener, casting an expert eye over some of the palace's current stock of 'exoticks'.

'There were three areas where exotics were displayed traditionally,' he explains. 'And we would be looking to put them back there: the space in front of the Lower Orangery, the Flower Quarter Garden and the walks and terraces of the Privy Garden.' The plants were brought out of their glasshouses during the summer months and set out – in their ornate pots – in well-spaced ranks. 'It is an exciting project,' confides Terry. Like almost everything else in the Hampton Court gardens it weaves together the elements of horticulture, history and public display.

NEEDLEWORK AND EMBROIDERY

Hampton Court has had a long and rich association with needlework. Queen Mary II's love of embroidery was almost obsessive. Certainly it drew especial notice from her contemporary biographer, Bishop Burnet. 'In all those hours that were not given to better employment,' he declared, 'she wrought with her own hands; and sometimes with so constant a diligence, as if she had been to earn her bread by it. It was a new thing, and looked like a sight, to see a Queen work so many hours a day.' She produced numerous carefully worked items – chair covers, screens, hangings. They were praised as being 'extremely neat and very well shadowed'. Many of them were once on show in the palace. They were exhibited together with pieces by another needle-plying Queen: Anne Boleyn.

When she was being courted by King Henry, Anne Boleyn embroidered a beautiful 'tester', or headboard, for the royal bed. It became – along with various other specimens of her handiwork – one of the sights of the palace. Sir Thomas Wyatt asserted that 'those who have seen at Hampton Court the rich and exquisite works by herself, for the greater part wrought by her own hand and needle, and also of her ladies, esteem them the most precious furniture that are to be

accounted amongst the most sumptuous that any prince may be possessed of.' But he considered even more precious, 'in the sight of God', those works 'which she caused her maids and those about her daily to work in shirts and smocks for the poor.'

A beautiful headpiece embroidered by Anne Boleyn is preserved at her family home, Hever Castle, in Kent, but – sadly – none of her work survives at Hampton Court. Several pieces reputedly

LEFT Heather Fordham, of the Royal School of Needlework, explains how it is done.
RIGHT In the library.

by Queen Mary II have, however, recently been put on show in the Queen's Closet. These thin strips of carefully worked cloth, intended as ornamental hangings, amply confirm the judgement that her work was 'neat and well shadowed'.

The great tradition of needlework at Hampton Court lives on. For the past twelve years the palace has been home not only to the Royal School of Needlework but also to the Embroiderers' Guild. Both institutions run popular courses and training programmes, and mount exhibitions. They draw students and apprentices from around the world. A professional apprenticeship at the RSN runs for three years; other courses can last for 'anything between one year and one day'.

In the RSN workroom on the upper, 'round window' storey of the Wren buildings, Heather Fordham presides over classes for a whole range of embroidery techniques. An atmosphere of informal concentration prevails, as the students – sitting around a large table – work steadily at mastering some specific technique.

'Our specialities are perhaps gold-thread embroidery, silk embroidery, black work, appliqué and "fine white",' explains Elizabeth Elvin, the school's Principal. 'There are many interesting connections between this sort of work and Hampton Court's history,' she says. 'Black work is sometimes called "Holbein stitch"; it is very much of the Tudor era.' Fine white was the stitch traditionally used for christening garments; it was doubtless used for the robe of the future Edward VI when, as a newborn infant, he was paraded around Hampton Court prior to his baptism in the Chapel.

Tina Soliss in the RSN workroom.

Claire Hanham mapping out a design.

Although much of the training provided by the RSN is traditional, new techniques are not ignored. 'As part of their training we teach our apprentices how to design patterns on a computer,' says Elizabeth.

The concentration of the country's two leading needlework institutions at Hampton Court is beneficial. 'We complement each other,' explains Elizabeth. 'Interest has grown in recent years. Certainly there is now a much greater awareness of what hand embroidery is all about.' The palace, moreover, provides a very attractive setting. 'People love coming to Hampton Court.'

As one regular American visitor to the RSN summer courses put it, 'To have that school in this setting could not be better; it's so inspiring seeing the flowers in the gardens each morning.' The school has not, however, yet revived the custom of sitting out in Queen Mary's bower to work – and gossip – in the open air.

RESTORATION

The maintenance of an important historic building poses a range of challenges. Ill-informed or insensitive restoration work can damage not only its character but also its structure, sometimes irretrievably. A thorough knowledge of a building's original materials, structure and function is necessary in order to inform all maintenance decisions.

At Hampton Court much of this knowledge is provided by Jonathan Foyle, the Assistant Curator of Historic Buildings, who has responsibility for both Hampton Court and Kew palaces. He combines archaeology and architectural history in his analyses of the buildings, in order to inform maintenance work. He gives advice about the correct materials to use and the appropriateness of proposed schemes.

Recently he has been involved with the major conservation work being carried out on the great South Front of Wren's wing. Having restored the King's Apartments and the Privy Garden beyond them, it seemed appropriate to complete the scene by restoring the façade between them. 'The South Front has been cleaned, the sash windows – some of the earliest in the country – have been restored and repainted,' Jonathan explains. 'Cleaning presented no particular problem, but painting was another matter.' It was clear to the curators at

Jonathan Foyle in front of the oriel window in the Great Hall.

Hampton Court that the window frames were the wrong colour. In recent times they had been painted a bright white, which stood out in a rather glaring contrast against the red brickwork.

'We wanted to discover what the original paint scheme had been,' says Jonathan. 'Paint sampling is an interesting discipline. You have to locate the oldest window, and then take a sample of paint from it. A seventeenth-century window might have between thirty and forty layers of paint on it.' The sample is sent to the laboratory where it is put under a powerful microscope and subjected to ultraviolet treatment in an effort to discover the pigments used in the earliest layers. This information is then fed back to inform the choice of paint used for the restoration. In the end an off-white, slightly darker in tone than the white it replaced, was decided upon. The effect upon the building's appearance is subtle but telling. This brings the façade another step closer to Wren's original vision.

Although physical evidence is important, documentary records often provide the vital clues, especially for the more transitory elements of design. Amongst the papers relating to the building of Wren's wing, Jonathan found a reference to red ochre being applied to the stonework around the relief carving over the windows. Any visible trace of redness had long since disappeared, but the reference was intriguing and was confirmed by chemical analysis of the stonework. It was decided to restore the ochre. 'It has a very striking effect,' says Jonathan 'It makes the actual carving stand out much more distinctly.' And, once again, it is an effect that Christopher Wren originally intended and William and Mary enjoyed.

Jonathan has found evidence of colour washes being used elsewhere in the palace. Wolsey, he has learnt, would often paint red-tinted lime wash over the whole surface of a brick wall to enhance its colour. And on important walls, such as the west

end of the Chapel, he would pick out the black-brick patterning – or 'diaper work' – with an additional coat of coal dust.

Jonathan spends a lot of time staring at brick walls. 'Brick typology is one of the growing areas of architectural history,' he says. A great deal can be learnt from the size, colour and make-up of a brick. And the very detailed building records relating to Hampton Court often allow one to trace a particular consignment of bricks from the kiln to their place in a palace wall. 'Sometimes,' Jonathan explains, 'we will make a schematic map of a wall surface, and examine every brick in it to see what is original and what is a replacement.'

Major restoration schemes frequently have unexpected benefits. When scaffolding is erected it allows curators to inspect inaccessible places in close detail. Recent work on the roof of the Great Hall provided Jonathan and his colleagues with an opportunity to search for traces of the great louvred opening that once rose like a Gothic pinnacle from the middle of the roof, allowing smoke out of the hall and light in. The structure, known only from old engravings, has long vanished but the curators were able to discover traces in the beam work that suggested exactly where the vent had been located, and what its dimensions would have been.

Such close scrutiny of the palace fabric can also lead to interesting new discoveries. Jonathan Foyle's examination of the brickwork on the outside walls of the Great Hall suggested to him that the great oriel window at the east end of the Hall might not be of a part with the rest of the building. 'It didn't seem to fit in with the rest of the Hall,' he explains. All sorts of minor architectural details aroused his

Adrian Phillips is Maintenance Manager of the South Front restoration.

Jonathan Foyle gets to know the palace fabric.

suspicion. The string course running along the side of the building takes a curious dip when it reaches the window. And the whole way in which the window attaches to the Hall is ungainly.

Although the current historical consensus holds that Henry VIII built the Great Hall and the elaborately carved oriel window, Foyle was prompted to ask whether perhaps he didn't merely adapt and extend Wolsey's existing scheme – and appropriate his existing window. A geological examination of the stone used in the window proved inconclusive. The very strong stylistic similarities, however, between the carving of the Hampton Court window and the oriel window built by Wolsey for the hall at Christ Church,

Oxford, were more persuasive, especially as the two master masons responsible for the elaborate tracery and vaulting of the Oxford window were both dead by the time Henry took over the running of Hampton Court. It would seem that the design of both could have been borrowed from Bath Abbey. Wolsey was Bishop of Bath and Wells between 1518 and 1523 and the designer of this vault at Bath was the business partner of the architect at Wolsey's Hampton Court.

Jonathan's findings will be published in due course, and will doubtless provoke their fair share of controversy and debate, but they remain a telling example of Hampton Court's continuing ability to reveal secrets and stimulate enquiries. The past lives on – sometimes hidden, sometimes revealed – in the very fabric of the palace.

CHAPTER 6

A ROYAL WELCOME

*T*he first Hanoverian King, George I, spent little time in England and, hence, even less at Hampton Court. Nevertheless he did visit the palace soon after his arrival in the country, and found there an escape from the perplexing pressures of London court life. To welcome him, the 'Diana' statue (as the Arethusa statue was now misnamed) was embellished by the court sculptor, Richard Osgood, with 'two large sea horses and two large Tritons to spout water'. And the Lion Gates, begun by Queen Anne as a northern entrance to the palace, were rather hastily finished off. Although the massive piers were all but complete, no actual gates had been made to fit between them. A fine pair designed by Tijou were, however, found elsewhere in the grounds and hastily erected. The result – as can still be seen – is not very happy: the elegant, low gates are sadly out

OPPOSITE The Queen's Dressing Room and Bathroom, set up as if for a royal bath. ABOVE The Wilderness.

of scale with the giant piers. Defoe considered the effect 'pitiful'. King George, however, does not seem to have taken notice of it.

According to contemporary accounts the King, once closeted at the palace, dispensed with both duty and ceremony. He refused to allow his principal courtiers into the King's Bedchamber to assist with his toilette. He spent 'many hours of the day in the sweet companionship of his ugly fat companions [Madame Schulenburg and Madame Kilmansegge], who cut out figures in paper for this royal diversion, while he, forgetful of the cares of state, lit his pipe and smoked placidly, now and then laughing and clapping his hands when Schulenburg had, in cutting out a figure, hit on some peculiarity of feature or figure in a courtier or minister'.

Despite such pleasant diversions, the King cared little for England. His grasp of English was slight and his understanding of the country limited. On his return to Hanover in the summer of 1716 he left his son, the Prince of Wales, as Regent, with permission to reside at Hampton Court. The Prince and his wife (the future George II and Queen Caroline) spent a happy season at the palace. The Queen's Apartments, left largely unfinished since the death of Mary II, were decorated for their use.

The Queen's Drawing Room had already been painted by Verrio but they fitted out the others: the Guard Chamber, the Presence Chamber, the Public Dining Room and the Bedchamber. The work fell largely to John Vanbrugh, the playwright and architect, who had become associated with Wren as an officer of His Majesty's Works. He worked in a new style of bold simplicity, still to be seen in the Queen's Presence Chamber, and in the magnificent, bare Guard Chamber, with its stark, sculptural cornice – and its comical fireplace (carved by Gibbons) showing two grotesque Yeomen of the Guard.

A more conventional scheme of decoration was allowed elsewhere. The ceiling of the Bedchamber was painted by James Thornhill, with a scene of Dawn dispelling Night and Sleep. On the cove of the ceiling he added medallion portraits of George I, the Prince and Princess, and their nine-year-old son, Frederick.

Aside from these State Rooms, the young royal couple also prepared two sets of private chambers for themselves. The Princess's ran along the inner enfilade of the east range, looking in upon Fountain Court. The Prince had his private apartments at the northeastern corner of the block.

That summer at Hampton Court the young Prince and Princess gathered about themselves a court of their own. The wit and beauty of their assembly were considered to be in sharp contrast to

The Lion Gate with its massive piers.

the dullness of the King's. The German element was combined with the English. Lord Stanhope, the future Earl of Chesterfield, was one of the Prince's Gentlemen of the Bedchamber, Lord Hervey was also in attendance, as was Charles Churchill, brother of the Duke of Marlborough. The Princess's ladies-in-waiting were celebrated in the poetry of Pope and Swift. They included the beautiful Mary Bellenden and 'Dear Molly' Lepell, and the no less lovely Mrs Howard, who became established at court as the Prince's acknowledged mistress.

Under the direction of the Prince and Princess of Wales, Hampton Court became once more a scene of gaiety. That summer was remembered by all who enjoyed it as a special time. Mornings were passed with boating parties on the river. At noon the Prince and Princess would dine in public, before the court, waited upon by the ladies-in-waiting. In the afternoon the Princess saw company in her Drawing Room or retired to her private apartments to read or write letters. In the early evenings she would walk with her ladies in the gardens. The arbours and walks offered an ideal setting for flirtation – 'frizalation' as the courtiers termed it. The little pavilions around the new bowling green were a favourite evening resort for card parties; each was fitted out as a miniature drawing room. But it was the high spirits of Miss Bellenden and Miss Lepell, and the gracious social tact of Mrs Howard, that seem to have bound the company together in good fellowship.

The Prince and Princess returned to Hampton Court the following summer, but the gaiety of the previous year could not be repeated. The King was with them. And his ponderous influence seems to have cast a pall over proceedings. This both caused, and was exacerbated by, a growing tension between him and his son. The King, it seems, had come to

A painting of George I from Kneller's studio.

resent his son's popularity and his social reputation.

Pope records the sad state of the court at this time. 'Our gallantry and gaiety have been great sufferers by the rupture of the two courts here,' he wrote to Lady Mary Wortley Montagu; 'scarce any ball, assembly, basset-table, or any place where two or three are gathered together. No lone house in Wales, with a rookery, is more contemplative than Hampton Court. I walked there the other day by the moon, and met no creature of quality but the King, who was giving audience all alone to the birds under the garden wall.'

Before the summer was over the Prince and Princess removed from Hampton Court, and their breach with the King became official. Having banished his son from the delights of the palace, the King made a determined effort to enjoy the place himself. In 1718 he held full court at Hampton Court, and embarked on a most uncharacteristic round of royal entertaining. He held assemblies and threw balls. Every available space from the Cartoon Gallery to the tennis court was pressed into service for these gatherings. He dined before his court in the Public Dining Room. And, taking his new expansiveness to unimagined limits, he fitted out the Great Hall as a theatre.

Seven plays were performed for his pleasure, including Shakespeare's *Hamlet* and *Henry VIII* and Ben Jonson's *Volpone*. Although it is uncertain quite how much the King really understood of Shakespeare's text, it is recorded that he laughed at a line in *Henry VIII* about how the King's ministers liked to claim credit for their master's ideas. Perhaps it had been explained to him beforehand. The rest of the audience was in the awkward position of having to take their cue from the King. As one of the actors recorded, the spectators were 'under the restraint of a circle where laughter or applause raised higher than a whisper would be stared at'. This restraint inevitably had a 'melancholy effect upon the impatient vanity' of some of the star performers.

Although the stage was left in place when the court departed in November, King George's experiment in sociability was not repeated. He had no aptitude for court life, and he was doubtless relieved to heal the breach with his son. They embraced, in a public reconciliation, on St George's Day, 1720. However, the King and Queen returned infrequently in the last seven years of his reign.

The King, however, did effect one significant change to the management of Hampton Court: he sacked Sir Christopher Wren. Wren's work as Surveyor General had been increasingly taken over by commissioners during the course of George I's reign. Nevertheless there seems to been some pressure, either political or personal, to remove Wren from the office. In 1718 he was dismissed at the age of eighty-six. Various charges of mismanagement were brought against him, but he answered that he could not be held responsible for acts carried out by the commissioners, and if there really were charges to be met they should face them. He ended his petition with the plea, 'as I am dismiss'd, having worn out (by God's mercy) a long life in the Royal Service, and having made some figure in the world, I hope it will be allowed me to die in peace'. He lived on for five more years in his house on the Green, although he died at his London home in St James's Street. His replacement as Surveyor General was a time-server called William Benson. He held the office for only a year.

DIVERSIONS AND ALARMS

George II came to the throne in 1727. He soon brought Hampton Court back within the fold of royal favour. He went to the palace in the July of 1728, and thereafter part of every summer was spent at Hampton Court, up until the death of Queen Caroline in 1737. During the course of this decade many small improvements were made, Tudor windows were altered, Tudor fireplaces refitted. Three rooms in the Queen's State Apartments were redecorated in the latest styles. Verrio's murals in the Queen's Drawing Room, which were not to George II's taste, were covered up with green damask. The murals were not uncovered until 1899.

Queen Caroline took a keen interest in religious matters. She liked to engage in weekly theological

discussions with her Chaplain, Samuel Clarke. As a setting for her daily devotions, she had built an octagonal domed Oratory as part of her private apartments.

To enhance the grandeur of her state rooms, the staircase approach, which until then had been left merely panelled and whitewashed, was refurbished. The stairway itself was, like that to the King's Apartments, graced with a wrought-iron balustrade by Tijou. The walls were painted by the new court architect and decorator, William Kent, with what one critic described as 'scroll work and a few unmeaning figures'. In the cornice the royal monograms were set. The staircase was not Kent's only contribution to the palace décor. In 1731 the

The Queen's Private Drawing Room with its crimson flock wallpaper.

King and Queen's second son, William Augustus, who was Duke of Cumberland, was ten; he became entitled to his own suite of rooms within the palace, and to his own household staff. Kent was asked to convert some of the Tudor state rooms on the east range of Clock Court into a set for the young royal Duke – with a Presence Chamber, a Bedchamber and Withdrawing Room. Although the rooms of what is still called 'The Cumberland Suite' are generally distinguished by their Georgian elegance and lightness, Kent did introduce some interesting 'archaeological' details. In a conscious echo of

Tudor style he decorated the ceiling of the Duke's Presence Chamber with plaster pendants. In the Queen's Gallery, Mantegna's *Triumphs of Caesar* were taken down and replaced with a scarcely less martial set of tapestries depicting the history of Alexander the Great.

Externally, too, he maintained the Tudor theme of Wolsey's palace. Rather than seeking to harmonize his new work with Wren's buildings, he created a mock 'gothick' look for his façade, and for the gateway leading through into Fountain Court. According to Horace Walpole, though, the decision

The Queen's Private Oratory.

to do this was made at the last moment: Kent had originally intended to use a colonnaded façade, similar to Wren's on the southern side of Clock Court, but he was overruled by the then Prime Minister, Sir Robert Walpole. The work was finished in 1732, and that date set above the gateway.

The Queen for her part directed her energies to the garden. The giant semi-circle of the Great Fountain Garden, which she looked down on from her rooms on the East Front, was replanted yet again, under her direction. The decorative element was simplified still further. The twelve small fountains were removed, leaving only the large fountain in the centre. The whole area was divided into four vast and simple lawns. For architectural decoration she relied on radiating avenues of yew, shaped into trim obelisks. It was a style that Pope satirized nimbly in his lines on Lord Burlington:

> *Tired of the scene parterre and fountains yield,*
> *He finds at last, he better likes a field...*

> *One boundless green or flourished carpet views*
> *With all the mournful family of yews.*

Something of the mournful character of the yews seems to have communicated itself to the court. Certainly the merriment of the fabled summer of 1716 was now a distant memory. Miss Bellenden and Miss Lepell were married and departed. 'Frizalation, flirtation, and dangleation' (whatever that might have been) were no more. Mrs Howard was still there. She received a visit from the King at precisely nine o'clock each evening. The Queen exacted a modest revenge upon her rival by making her, as a lady of the bedchamber, perform her menial duties on bended knee.

Hunting became the principal daytime diversion of the court. The King and his children – daughters as well as sons – rode after the hounds; the Queen, accompanied by Lord Hervey, followed in a coach. In the evening cards were played. There were fixed moments, too, of court ceremony: levées in the State Bedchamber, receptions in the Presence Chamber and drawing rooms, and dining in the Public Dining Room. Of other amusement there was little. In October 1731, however, the King did invite the Actors' Company to make use of the stage in the Great Hall. But they performed for only one night.

Lord Hervey, writing to a friend in 1733, gives a vivid sketch of court life in all its monotony.

King George II by David Morier.

I will not trouble you with any account of our occupations at Hampton Court. No mill-horse ever went in a more constant track, for the day of the week, and a watch for the hour of the day, you may inform yourself fully, without any other intelligence but your memory, of every transaction within the verge of the Court. Walking, chaises, levees and audiences fill the morning; at night the King plays at commerce and backgammon, and the Queen at quadrille, where poor Lady Charlotte [de Roucy] runs her usual nightly gauntlet – the Queen pulling her hood, Mr Schutz sputtering in her face, and the Princess Royal rapping her knuckles, all at a time. It was in vain she fled from persecution for her religion: she suffers for her pride what she escaped for her faith; undergoes in a drawing room what she dreaded from the Inquisition, and will die a martyr to a Court, though not to a church.

The Duke of Grafton takes his nightly opiate of lottery, and sleeps as usual between the Princesses Amelia and Carolina; Lord Grantham strolls from one room to another (as Dryden says), 'like some discontented ghost that oft appears and is forbid to speak,' and stirs himself about, as people stir a fire, not with any design, but in hopes to make it burn brisker, which his lordship constantly does, to no purpose, and yet tries as constantly as if it had ever once succeeded.

At last the King comes up; the pool finishes, and everybody has this dismission: their Majesties retire to Lady Charlotte and my Lord Lifford; the Princesses, to Bilderbec and Lony; my Lord Grantham to Lady Frances and Mr Clark; some to supper, and some to bed; and thus (to speak in the scripture phrase) the evening and the morning make the day.

This happy round of tedium was, however, broken in upon during the late summer of 1736. Relations between the King and Queen and their eldest son, Frederick, Prince of Wales, had been deteriorating for some years. The Prince had been born in 1707 and brought up in Hanover until he was twenty. He had developed into a conceited and objectionable young man, even by the standards of Hanoverian princes. He scorned his parents, ridiculed his siblings and lived entirely for himself. Queen Caroline kept up a constant stream of lamentation on the subject of her first-born. The King pretended he did not exist, often walking past him at court receptions as though he 'filled a void of space'.

In 1736 the Prince married Augusta, the daughter of the Duke of Saxe-Gotha. The King offered his son an allowance of £50,000 a year on the occasion. But the Prince refused it and petitioned Parliament for an increase. His request was refused, but the incident served to worsen relations still further. Nor were the King and Queen much impressed with their new daughter-in-law. They considered her a sad specimen. When the news broke that she had become pregnant, it was greeted with surprise, bordering almost on disbelief. The King and Queen's concern was only increased by the Prince's evasiveness on the subject. He would give them no information about when the child might be due, and he instructed his wife to be similarly obtuse. The Queen was prepared to believe her son capable of anything. She thought he might even be falsely proclaiming a non-existent pregnancy 'with the intention of adding to his own importance, or imposing on them with a suppositious child'.

In an effort to prevent any such scheme, the King instructed Sir Robert Walpole to order the Prince and Princess to come to Hampton Court for the confinement. The message was delayed as it was thought that the accouchement was still some months off. The Prince and Princess, nevertheless, came to Hampton Court that summer. They were lodged in the Prince of Wales suite at the north end of the east range. The Princess spent some time in the company of the Queen, but Prince Frederick seems to have avoided his family.

On the evening of 31 July 1737, the Princess dined with the King and Queen in the Public Dining Room. After the meal she retired to her own rooms to rejoin the Prince. The rest of the court dispersed to their card parties in the various chambers and private suites. While the usual round of play and gossip got under way, a less expected drama began to unfold in the princely apartments.

Almost as soon as she returned to her own suite, the Princess went into labour. The Prince had a mad determination that the child should not be born at Hampton Court, if only to confound his parents' will. He at once ordered his servants to bring round his coach. He ordered the poor Princess to prepare for departure. Supported by her dancing-master and one of the Prince's equerries, she was led downstairs. In tears she begged to be allowed to remain, but the Prince urged her on with cries of 'Courage, courage!'

They made the safety of the coach undetected, and then drove off towards London, and St James's Palace. The journey was a nightmare. The Princess was attended by two of her dressers, by the Prince's mistress – Lady Archibald Hamilton – and by his valet-de-chambre, who was presented as being a surgeon and 'man midwife'.

The court knew nothing of the drama until one of the Prince's servants arrived from London back at Hampton Court the following morning with the news that the Princess had given birth to a baby girl. At first the news was not believed. It was too extraordinary. But after a search of the Prince of Wales's suite revealed that he had indeed departed, amazement gave way to anger.

The King rather unjustly scolded the Queen, telling her: 'You see now, with all your wisdom, how they have outwitted you. This is all your fault. There is a false child will be put upon you, and how will you answer it to all your children?' The Queen hurried at once to London to view the doubtful baby. She was positively relieved to discover the infant 'a little rat of a girl, about the bigness of a good large toothpick case'. If it had been 'a brave, large

fat jolly boy' she would have suspected a 'juggle'. But the 'poor little ugly she-mouse' could only be the real thing. (She grew up to be a most unmouselike woman, and the Duchess of Brunswick.)

The King refused to see either his son or the new grandchild. When the Prince suggested a visit to Hampton Court he was repulsed. As a final insolence the Prince then published an edited account of the King's letters to him, making out that he had been a model son very badly treated by an irrational father. The King retaliated by announcing that the Prince and Princess must leave St James's Palace.

Even by the poor standards of Hanoverian family relations the rift was bitter. It was, nevertheless, eclipsed soon afterwards. At the end of that summer, soon after the court left Hampton

Hampton Court Palace and its gardens in the mid eighteenth century.

Court, Queen Caroline fell ill. She never recovered. On her deathbed the Queen sent a message of reconciliation to her recalcitrant son. After her death King George, though he ruled for a further twenty-three years, never spent another summer at the palace. He would make occasional visits there, with his mistress of the moment, and walk about the gardens, or wander through the rooms, but he did not take up residence again.

The disrespectful Frederick predeceased him, dying in 1751, but not before he had produced a son and heir. It is told that King George was once walking with this boy in the Long Gallery at Hampton Court when some chance remark or act enraged him. In old age the King's temper had become both short and violent. He was apt to kick his wig around the room at the mildest provocation. On this occasion he boxed his grandson's ears. The reverberations of the blow continue to this day.

GRACE AND FAVOUR

George III, as the young grandson became, never resided at Hampton Court. It is uncertain whether he made a formal resolution to abandon the palace, or whether the break occurred unnoticed and by degrees. It is said that the unhappy memory of that grandparental chastisement set the new King against the place. Or perhaps it was a sense of economy that persuaded him on his course of action.

Certainly very soon after his accession, in 1760, George III began to remove items of use and decoration from Hampton Court to his other residences. All the 'kitchen goods' were taken up to Westminster 'for his service' at the Coronation. They were not brought back. The Raphael cartoons were taken down and transported to Windsor. Other treasures followed.

The palace itself did not stand empty. An extensive staff was maintained – housekeepers, gardeners, gamekeepers and workmen. And beyond these domestic officials and servants there were other residents too. It had long been a problem at Hampton Court, as at other royal palaces, to prevent unscrupulous individuals from taking over apartments during the court's absence and 'squatting' in them. The ruses employed in such cases were many: impoverished courtiers, assigned a room for a brief visit to court, would invent excuses to prolong their stay indefinitely; others would beg the Lord Chamberlain, or bribe the housekeeper, for the temporary grant of a few rooms, and then surreptitiously add adjacent rooms to build up a substantial suite.

Since the time of Henry VIII almost every English monarch had issued exasperated edicts, denouncing such practices and threatening heavy penalties. Nothing, however, seemed to avail. George III perceived that it might be better to regularize and direct the practice rather than struggle against it. He resolved to grant the vacant rooms at Hampton Court to tenants of his own choosing. He instituted a formal scheme of 'grace and favour lodging', rent-free accommodation in the gift of the King. Applications had to be granted by the Lord Chamberlain, who would then send a note of authorization to the palace housekeeper, specifying the particular suite of rooms to be occupied. All the rooms around the Base and Clock Courts, the floors above the Royal Apartments, and some of the outlying buildings were designated as lodgings.

Very soon most of the palace was filled with private families and individuals, favoured servants of the Crown, heroes of His Majesty's forces, relics of public figures, and even impoverished writers. In 1776 Samuel Johnson applied to Lord Hertford, the Lord Chamberlain, for a set of rooms:

My Lord,

Being wholly unknown to your lordship, I have only this apology to make for presuming to trouble you with a request – that a stranger's petition, if it cannot be easily granted, can be easily refused. Some of the apartments at Hampton Court are now vacant, in which I am encouraged to hope that, by application to your lordship, I may obtain a residence. Such a grant would be considered by me as a great favour; and I hope, to a man who has had the honour of vindicating his Majesty's government, a retreat in one of his houses may be not improperly or unworthily allowed. I therefore request that your lordship will be pleased to grant such rooms in Hampton Court as shall seem proper to,

My lord,
Your lordship's most obedient and humble servant,
Sam. Johnson.

The request, however, was turned down. The apartments had already been taken. During these early years no particular precedence seems to have been given to those in need. Hannah More, the bluestocking and social reformer, on a visit to Hampton Court in 1770, was moved to note that the majority of the apartments were 'occupied by people of fashion, mostly of quality; and that people of large fortune will solicit for them'. The system, moreover, was open to abuse. Some of those who secured rooms were not above subletting them for money. Others, having been granted rooms, never – or barely – used them. The Lord Chamberlain inveighed against these abuses; but the frequency of his proscriptions suggests that he was often ignored.

By filling up the palace with grace-and-favour residents and denuding the State Apartments (and kitchens) of some of their more important contents, George III rapidly made it impossible for the court to return to Hampton Court. For the King to take up residence again would necessitate an upheaval, and an expense, not to be easily countenanced.

A minor upheaval was occasioned in 1795 when the King's cousin, William V, Prince of Orange and Stadtholder of Holland, was obliged to flee the Netherlands in the wake of their invasion by French revolutionary troops. George III at once offered him the hospitality of Hampton Court. Several existing tenants had to move their apartments in order to accommodate the Stadtholder, his family and their suite. They were installed in the Queen's Private Apartments along the south range of Fountain Court, and lived there for seven years.

It has been suggested that the shaded avenue under the Tilt Yard wall is known by the curious name of the 'Frog Walk' on account of having been the favoured promenade of the Stadtholder's female relatives: the Dutch *fraus* or *frows* being ungenerously anglicized as 'frogs'. Although the King made a few courtesy visits to his cousin – and occasionally hunted in the park – he never spent the night at the palace.

Hampton Court had become even more accessible in 1753 with the construction of a bridge over the Thames just beyond its gates. The first bridge, a wonderful rococo construction with seven pronounced humps, had not been practical for vehicles, and it was replaced in 1778. (The present bridge – which stands on the same site – was designed by Sir Edwin Lutyens and opened in 1930.)

Despite its decline as a royal residence Hampton Court Palace was not completely neglected. Conservation work was intermittently carried out. The gatehouse on the west front had fallen into disrepair and had become a safety hazard. It was partially dismantled and rebuilt, although at a reduced scale. The top two storeys were left off, and the leaden cupolas and gilded vanes that once adorned its four octagonal turrets were also lost. Other minor alterations were effected. The Great Hall was tidied up, the old stage was removed and the roof was repaired. The majestic space could be appreciated once again uncluttered by scaffolding.

Such considerations were coming increasingly to the fore. Hampton Court had always existed as a wonder to be visited. As court life retreated from the palace, during the later years of George II's life and throughout the reign of George III, it became more than ever a showplace. At this stage arrangements for viewing were quite informal. Application – and payment – was made to the Lady Housekeeper. Her deputy, or some other minor servant, would then escort visitors through the State Rooms. The money taken over a year was substantial, providing a useful supplement to the Housekeeper's official income.

Some discerning visitors found much of interest to admire among the neglected treasures of the palace. Horace Walpole, who lived nearby at

Grace-and-favour lodgings overlooked Fountain Court.

Strawberry Hill, and who had several relatives living in grace-and-favour apartments, was a frequent caller. He studied the art and architecture with keen appreciation. Hannah More on her visit was less impressed. She was shown a lot of dubious relics and antiquities, including an 'ordinary room full of... cane tables, chairs etc.' said to have belonged to Cardinal Wolsey. Also exhibited at this time was one of the Cardinal's shoes, although, as one critic recalled, since 'the upper leather had been renewed at one time, and the sole at another, its claim to reverence was of a somewhat impalpable kind'.

The palace gardens were under the care of Lancelot 'Capability' Brown. He had been appointed Royal Gardener at Hampton Court in 1750 by George II, and maintained in his post by the next King. Although George III asked him to 'improve' the gardens along modern lines, Brown very sensibly demurred, 'out of respect to himself and his profession'. Nevertheless the prevalent fashion for the 'natural' was allowed to take hold in some areas. The yew and holly obelisks in the Great Fountain Garden were allowed to grow unchecked and untrimmed, and the Wilderness was left to turn into something approximating to its name. Amongst this general policy of *laissez-faire*, however, Brown was responsible for one notable horticultural addition to the palace. He planted the Great Vine.

The process begun by George III continued during the reign of George IV, the palace serving the twin functions of a residence for Crown servants or their dependants and a showcase for Crown treasures. It became jokingly known as the 'quality poor house'. The elderly inhabitants gave the place a hushed and retiring tone. Lady Mornington, the mother of the Duke of Wellington and of the Marquess of Wellesley, had rooms in what had once been the Prince of Wales's suite, at the northeastern corner of Wren's block. She was often visited by her two illustrious sons. The victor of Waterloo is credited with having christened the sheltered nook on the east front of the palace (to the right of the gateway as you pass from Fountain Court out into the garden) 'Purr Corner'. It was a favourite spot with many of the old ladies of the palace. They would sit in its sun-filled shelter and gossip away the hours, their low tones suggesting the purring of so many cats – at least to the Iron Duke.

The palace still continued to be visited but little provision was made for the interested public. One account of 1823 gives a vivid picture of the sad condition of the State Apartments. 'These princely halls have come to be almost as silent as their dead master's tomb. They have nothing to echo back but the hurried footstep of a single domestic, who passes through them daily, to wipe away the dust of their untrodden floors, only that it may collect again; or the unintelligible jargon of a superannuated dependant, as he describes to a few straggling visitors (without looking at either) the objects of art that have been deposited in them, like treasures in a tomb.'

George IV confined his attention to the park. He substantially expanded the stud farm which had existed to the north of the Long Water in the Home Park since the time of William III. He improved the paddocks and the stable blocks, and increased the bloodstock. Although the stud no longer functions, the Stud House, which was remodelled in the 1830s, still stands, and is used as a private residence.

The palace itself George IV ignored, except for plunder. He removed the four statues – of Flora, Ceres, Diana and Pomona – from the south front,

The Stud House, the centre for royal horse breeding in Georgian times.

together with all the marble and lead statues from the Privy Garden, and transported them to Windsor. He also took from the Privy Garden terrace the great marble urns sculpted by Edward Pearce and Caius Cibber.

Despite such depredations a tenuous regal connection was maintained by the presence nearby of the Duke of Clarence, the King's brother and the future William IV. In 1798 he was made Ranger of Bushy Park. He resided at Bushy House and established a farm for himself in the attached parkland. He entered too into the social life of the place and allowed himself to be made president of a dining club that met each month in the Toy Inn, just outside the palace gates. Many of the other members of the 'Toy Club' resided in apartments in the palace.

This knowledge of the palace, its surroundings and inhabitants, was significant when the Duke acceded to the throne in 1830. He seems to have conceived the idea of establishing the palace on a rather better footing, as a museum of choice and curious works from the royal collection. He gave orders for hundreds of canvases to be brought from storage at other royal palaces and hung at Hampton Court. Many of them, however, according to one judge, were 'little more than rubbish'. Several additional State Rooms were now opened to accommodate them. He paid for the restoration of the sadly dilapidated King's Staircase, and he replaced the old face of Henry VIII's astronomical clock with one from St James's Palace.

The viewing of this and the other treasures remained, however, an unsatisfactory business. One contemporary connoisseur recalled being 'driven' through the rooms by one of the deputy-keeper's housemaids, who 'pointed out the pictures with a long stick, calling out, in a loud voice, at the same time, the names and the subjects and their painters...a procedure that allowed of little opportunity for studying or enjoying them'.

THE GREAT VINE

*I*n the glass-walled, centrally heated Vinery, at the western corner of the Pond Garden, grows the Great Vine. It is one of the sights of the palace, and probably the most famous vine in the world. It was planted in about 1768 by the celebrated garden designer Lancelot 'Capability' Brown. Brown was the Surveyor of the Gardens and Waters of Hampton Court during the reign of George III. He had lodgings on site in Wilderness House, and, if he did not actually put the young vine into the ground, he certainly oversaw its planting. Indeed, it was one of the few decisive improvements he made to the palace grounds during his tenure.

The vine is of the 'Black Hamburg' variety and was put in to produce dessert grapes for the royal table. The plant came from a cutting of a large vine growing at Valentines, a manor house at Ilford in Essex. It prospered immediately and the Vinery very soon had to be enlarged. Space, however, was limited as the vine house was at the angle of two buildings. The bole of the vine, which had originally stood outside the walls of the Vinery in accordance with common practice, became enclosed by the new structure. But even this had – and has – no effect upon the vigour of the plant. It still spreads out as a great canopy across the sloping roof of the Vinery.

Gillian Cox, Keeper of the Great Vine, prepares for the harvest.

Various theories have been put forward to explain this exceptional growth and fecundity. One is that the vine's roots penetrated the palace cesspool. Another is that the roots had reached the nearby Thames. Gillian Cox, the Keeper of the Great Vine, is sceptical. 'I think the roots just go into the patch of ground outside the vine house,' she says. 'But it's a very fertile and well-watered plot.'

Large vines used to be a feature of the horticultural scene. 'In Victorian times,' she explains, 'the Hampton Court vine was one of twenty or thirty well-known vines in the country. They became tourist attractions.' When the Vinery was remodelled for a second time at the beginning of the twentieth century a special viewing area was constructed. None of the other vines have survived – most of them fell victim to neglect. But at Hampton Court the vine has always received the care and attention necessary to keep it both healthy and productive.

Since at least the 1850s the plant has had its own designated Keeper living on site. It is a position of great responsibility. 'There's a lot of history here,' says Gillian, 'and we don't want to lose it. No one would like to be remembered as the person who killed the Great Vine at Hampton Court. My husband sometimes jokes that if it did die, I'd be straight off to the Tower of London and...' She draws a finger across her throat. And who can say that he is wrong. The vine is one of the special wonders of the palace.

It certainly needs its own keeper. Looking after it is a full-time occupation. 'It's a bit like painting the Forth Bridge,' Gillian explains. 'The work goes on round the year, and then you are ready to begin again.' What with pruning, 'disbudding', 'stopping', 'training in', 'thinning out' and harvesting, there are few quiet periods in the year. Much of this work is a matter of 'curbing the vine's natural exuberance'. And, on top of the general round of care, there is other work in train. The earth inside the Vinery is currently being improved to provide better drainage.

Under such a regime the vine continues to thrive. It still yields about a thousand bunches each summer, close to what it produced in the mid-nineteenth century. 'Old vines are prone to overcropping,' explains Gillian, 'so it's important to control the size of the crop – to reduce the number of bunches and even to thin out individual bunches. If I left it to itself it would produce one great big crop, but then it would probably never fruit again – or, at least, fruit only very erratically.'

Thinning out the crop is a 'fiddly business', as grapes have to be taken out without rubbing the bloom off the rest of the bunch. 'It's important to try to keep the shape of the bunches,' says Gillian, 'so I thin them from the inside.' There are special vine-keeper's scissors for the task. But Gillian also uses a pencil to manoeuvre the bunches.

The grapes are usually harvested on August Bank Holiday – although a cold summer can put the date back a week or two. The bunches are no longer destined for the royal dessert table. Since 1935 they have been sold to visitors to the palace. They used to be on sale in the Vinery itself, but are now distributed from the palace shops. Until the 1960s the bunches were packaged in small baskets made by blind ex-servicemen at St Dunstan's; now they are wrapped in tissue paper and packed in cardboard cake-boxes. Gillian has to make the boxes up herself, helped by some of the other palace gardening staff who lend a hand during the busiest moment of the Vinery year.

The palace's vine-keepers clearly develop a special relationship with their plant. One of the previous incumbents at Hampton Court had his ashes sprinkled round the Vinery after his death – it is not recorded whether there was a bumper crop the next year. Gillian has developed her own rapport with her historic charge, but there are limits to the relationship. 'People often ask me if I talk to the vine,' she says. 'I have to admit that I don't, although when I'm struggling to get to a bunch that is just out of reach I do sometimes curse it.'

The Vine House with the Keeper's house adjacent.

TOURISM

'Hampton Court was built to impress and entertain,' says Donna Gelardi, the palace's Marketing Director. 'That was the way Cardinal Wolsey started it and Henry VIII took it on, and that's what we now try to do – impress and entertain our day visitors, our functions visitors, our visitors for events like the music festival and the flower show. We try to stay true to the original purpose of the palace.'

Nevertheless, all this entertainment and impressing has to be done to a budget. There are, of course, great financial pressures. As Dennis McGuinnes, Hampton Court's Deputy Director, explains, 'In April of 1998 Hampton Court, together with the four other Historic Royal Palaces, abandoned its status as a government agency and became a charitable trust. Now we have to pay for ourselves. We had been working towards that for the last five years, and I am confident that we will be able to manage it.'

The cost of maintaining and running the palace is enormous. Bruce Winton, the Financial Controller, estimates that it takes almost £9.5 million a year to keep the palace open. This sum has to be generated by revenue from the public.

The potential for raising money is great, but the constraints are many. 'Getting more people and more money into the palace are not necessarily the

Costumed interpreters help to bring the palace alive for a new generation of visitors.

aims of the game,' explains Winton. 'Our first stated goal as a charity is, in fact, the preservation and the maintenance of the palace for future generations. Our second goal is to open the palace to the current generation, to allow them in to see the palace. We are not a profit-making organization: everything we earn goes back into the palace. But we do always have this delicate balance between getting money in and maintaining the palace.'

As a result, running Hampton Court as a tourist attraction presents special challenges and special opportunities. Donna, who came to the palace from what she describes as a 'commercial background', admits to having spent her first six months in the job suffering from culture shock.

'Every time you come up with a commercial idea,' she says, 'you have to consider what it is going to mean to the palace not only in terms of wear and tear on the fabric of the building, but also in terms of what is very quaintly called the "status and dignity" of the palace. And that can be a very subjective thing: status and dignity mean different things to different people. So every proposal gets looked at in great detail.'

The Curator's Department acts as a check on the activities of the Commercial Department. 'They are there to ensure the conservation of the building,' explains Donna, 'and to maintain the authenticity of everything we do. Sometimes there is a clash, but in general things tend to work well.'

Areas such as corporate functions or special events work better for being limited and exclusive. 'We could have Hampton Court booked for corporate functions and events every night of the year,' says Donna, 'but we don't want to turn it into a "corporate venue". We want to preserve its specialness – after all that is one of its greatest selling points. A dinner at Hampton Court is a unique occasion.'

Special events present a certain temptation. 'The music festival and the Flower Show generate quite a sizeable percentage of the total income that the palace receives,' explains Bruce Winton. 'Unfortunately, they do cause a large amount of disruption to other visitors and also wear and tear on the fabric of the building and the gardens. It takes almost the whole year for the east gardens to recover from the flower show being there. And for the music festival we have to build an arena in the Base Court, which means that other visitors can't see the court in its entirety.'

Providing for the general public presents different challenges. Hampton Court is a Historic Royal Palace. It has rich and unique historical associations that few other buildings in Britain can rival, and yet – as Donna points out – history is all in the past. 'History is static,' she explains. 'We have to try to bring it – and the palace – to life.' It is the great achievement of all those involved with Hampton Court that this is done so triumphantly.

Hampton Court is now one of Britain's top tourist attractions. It is a member of the Association of Leading Visitor Attractions (ALVA), a group of thirty elite organizations each of which attracts over a million visitors a year. They meet regularly to discuss ideas and trends. With so many leisure activities on offer to the public it is a constant battle to maintain levels of interest.

At Hampton Court, there is a determination not to compromise in search of quick popularity. 'We are very fussy about what we do,' admits Donna. 'We wanted to bring life to the palace but we didn't want to turn it into a "theme park". After all, Hampton Court already has its theme – its history. We just have to make that accessible and understandable to visitors.'

Restoration projects – in Henry VIII's rooms, William III's apartments and the Privy Garden – together with the creation of special period 'routes' and recorded tours, have all helped to make the palace's varied history readily accessible and vivid. Everything has to be authentic, and true to its particular period. This, however, can lead to some interesting complications.

'One of the things we sometimes get complaints about,' explains Donna, 'is the lack of furniture in the Royal Apartments. We have to explain that this is historically accurate: royal rooms didn't have furniture in them, because if the monarch was there nobody else was allowed to sit down, and if monarchs were not in residence they would take all their furniture with them.' As Hampton Court doesn't have a King or Queen in residence, the aim is to present the palace as though the monarch had just left.

Nevertheless, it is not completely deserted. At Christmas there are special activities – jugglers, stilt-walkers and jesters. They are very popular, although Donna admits to some misgivings: 'We make sure they are as authentic as possible, but if the court wasn't sitting at Hampton Court at the time they wouldn't really have been around…'

The magnificent interior of the Banqueting House can provide a magical setting for important occasions.

Lucy Capito in her new Tudor finery welcomes some young visitors.

Amongst the more permanent living fixtures at Hampton Court are the 'costumed interpreters' – men and women in authentic period dress who provide guided tours of some of the State Apartments. The guides were introduced in 1992 and have proved a great success. As Anne Fletcher, the Head of Interpretation and Education, points out, 'They remind people that the palace was inhabited.'

Great care is taken in designing and making the costumes so that they are as authentic as possible – 'right down to the underwear'. They are designed and made by a specialist company. Patterns are based on old paintings and drawings as well as on surviving clothes from the period. Each costume has to be vetted by the palace's curatorial team, to approve its historical authenticity. Details of cut and colour are examined closely. 'Sumptuary legislation' laid down strict codes about what could and could not be worn at court. In Tudor times the colour purple could only be worn by the Queen, her daughters and a few intimate members of the royal circle. The height of headresses and the length of sleeves were all well regulated.

The authenticity of the costumes is important, and not only for the sake of historical accuracy. 'You don't feel at all self-conscious,' explains Lucy Capito, who works as a guide in the Tudor part of the palace. 'You feel right. You have complete confidence in the clothes. If they were made of old curtains it would be different.'

However, the costumed interpreters do not rely just on their outfits to bring the palace to life. All of them are very knowledgeable about the history of Hampton Court.

'They are not out-of-work actors, as many people assume,' says Donna of the guides. 'They tend to be historians with a specialist interest in the period that they are talking about. They don't have scripts; they put together their own tours. We do test them regularly to make sure that everything they are saying is factually accurate, but the key is that they have to be entertaining. They know how to incorporate all the little stories about the palace, the gossip of the time; they explain about the etiquette of the period – how to behave when in the presence of the monarch, or how to flirt in the sixteenth century.'

The palace presents peculiar problems when it comes to establishing authenticity. Because the building spans so many different periods – from the Tudor age to the era of William and Mary – different histories have to be kept in mind, and in order. 'We are very strict about these things,' explains Donna. 'We won't let people in Tudor costume go into the William III bit of the palace because that could never have happened, but William III costumes are allowed to go into the Tudor rooms, because the Tudor part of the palace was there in William III's time.'

Because changes have been made to Hampton Court throughout the centuries it has many histories and many levels of authenticity. There are perfectly preserved Tudor spaces, whole suites of rooms from the time of William and Mary, Georgian interiors and Victorian additions. Sometimes the period elements are separate, sometimes they are muddled together. All these different historical strands have to be kept in mind and – just as importantly – in order.

A tour of the Tudor Kitchens.

THE SALVAGE TEAM

For almost 370 years Hampton Court avoided serious fire. While other royal palaces – such as Whitehall – went up in flames, smoke continued to issue benignly from the chimneys at Hampton Court. Nevertheless, the potential danger was recognized – at least by some. In the early eighteenth century an enterprising engineer tried to convince Queen Anne to install a powerful new pumping engine at one of the ponds in Bushy Park, suggesting that it would not only make the palace fountains work better, but would also be a very useful resource in case of fire. The thrifty Queen, however, was not to be persuaded.

As the number of visitors to the palace increased during the course of the nineteenth century, so did anxiety about fire. In 1878 the Board of Works undertook a comprehensive review of the fire precautions at the palace. Amongst their provisions they instituted a volunteer Palace Fire Brigade, consisting of a Superintendent and eighteen men (six of them residents). The brigade was equipped with a smart steam-powered fire engine able to pump 700 gallons of water per minute up on to the roof of the building. The Board also laid a special fire-main on the roof, behind the parapet, so that firemen could deluge the top of the building from above.

The equipment was no sooner in place than it was called into action. Towards the end of the

Joe Cowell, the head of the Hampton Court Salvage Team, keeps an eye on training.

century two fires occurred within four years of each other. In 1882 a servant in one of the grace-and-favour lodgings above the Queen's Gallery knocked over a spirit stove on which she was making a cup of tea. She was able to raise the alarm at once, but the room caught fire. Prompt action by the Palace Fire Brigade ensured that the fire was soon brought under control. Only three rooms were damaged, and no works of art were lost. Unfortunately the servant, having raised the alarm, returned to the room to try to salvage some of her possessions and was overcome by fumes.

The fire of 1886 was more serious, although there was no loss of life. It started in the southwest corner of Chapel Court, when a servant left a lighted candle in a cupboard. Over forty rooms were destroyed in the conflagration, including Edward VI's former nursery quarters in the north range of the palace. Fire brigades arrived from all the neighbouring towns, and the men of 10th Hussars also lent their assistance to help bring the fire under control.

Both fires, despite the damage they caused, provided an opportunity for renovation and restoration. Later Georgian accretions could be eradicated, and the rooms returned to something closer to their Tudor aspect.

Although Hampton Court no longer has its own fire brigade, it does have a volunteer salvage team, made up of workers living in – or near – the palace. They are responsible for rescuing movable items of furniture and art during any emergency. When a leak was discovered in the ceiling of the Queen's Apartments, the salvage team was called in to remove the curtains and overmantel painting.

It is delicate work that requires training, practice and white gloves. Handling valuable pieces of art under pressure is taxing in itself, but becomes more so when it has to be done at giddy-making heights. Part of the salvage team's training programme includes regular work assembling and mounting the special four-storey scaffolding towers that are

Everything has to be handled with care.

used for reaching the ceilings of the double-height State Apartments. It is one of the sternest tests for new recruits to the team.

Sometimes, however, there is no time to use such elaborate equipment. Disasters have a habit of arriving unannounced. The two nineteenth-century conflagrations were minor compared to the terrible fire that broke out above the King's Apartments on Easter Monday 1986. It started in the early hours of the morning in a grace-and-favour apartment on the top floor of Wren's great block. It took hold in the area above the ceiling of the Cartoon Gallery before it was detected at around 5am and the alarm was raised.

The salvage team were the first people on the scene. Their memories of the event are still vivid. They dashed through the King's Apartments trying to locate the seat of the fire. They were alerted by the amount of smoke drifting along the corridors. When they reached the Cartoon Gallery, they looked up and saw that the ceiling was glowing red and the paint on it was bubbling. The fire, they realized, was above them. The ceiling might at any moment give way.

By great good fortune the tapestries based on Raphael's cartoons, which usually hung in the gallery, had been removed only days before for restoration. Nevertheless, there were several important pictures hanging in the room. The salvage team was able to remove them before the fire brigade arrived. After that the team divided into two and worked its way through the chambers on either side of the gallery, clearing the pictures and art works as it went.

The fire, meanwhile, had engulfed the whole of the third floor of the block, and although over 120 firemen were on site the situation was still critical. The salvage team heard the ceiling of the Cartoon Gallery crash down and then, moments after they had cleared the King's Privy Chamber, its ceiling collapsed too, spewing tons of molten lead and charred timber into the room. The great chandelier which hung from the middle of the ceiling, and which had been too difficult to remove, was buried beneath a heap of rubble.

The team worked throughout the day, bringing paintings and objects to safety as the fire brigade battled to overcome the fire. Some very large pieces and built-in fixtures had to be left *in situ*. But, amazingly, when the tally was taken at the end of the day only one painting, one small table, and one length of limewood carving had been completely

Gaining a head for heights is part of the training process that all new recruits to the team have to go through.

lost to the flames. The general damage, however, was extensive. Much basic fabric – panelling and plaster – was consumed. Besides the Cartoon Gallery and the Privy Chamber, the Withdrawing Room and Eating Room were also badly damaged. Fire, smoke and water had all taken their toll, even on the objects rescued from the fire. And Lady Gale, the grace-and-favour resident in whose apartments the fire had begun, died in the conflagration, asphyxiated by the smoke.

The Queen visited the palace during the course of the day, to witness the devastation and to thank the service crews for their efforts in saving so much. Several members of the salvage team were subsequently awarded medals.

As with the previous fires, the disaster – for all its awfulness – proved both an opportunity and a lesson. Soon after the process of restoring the damaged rooms and artefacts began it was decided that the apartments, rather than being laid out as they had been with a general display of seventeenth-century decorative art, should be returned to their original 1700 form. They should be made to look as Wren and William III had intended.

The task of restoration was prodigious. Pictures needed to be cleaned, tapestries to be restored. Parts of some Grinling Gibbons carvings had to be replaced. The shattered fragments of the rock-crystal chandelier were rescued from the debris in the King's Privy Chamber and painstakingly reassembled. Much research was needed to determine how the rooms had originally been.

The scene of devastation after the fire.

The Salvage Team is made up of volunteers based in or near to the palace; they train together regularly.

After just six years, however, the Queen was able to return to Hampton Court to reopen the King's Apartments in all their new splendour. They exist now as a wonderful record not only of late-seventeenth-century taste, but of late-twentieth-century craftsmanship and care.

The fire has also prompted further refinements in the procedures and practices for dealing with such disasters. Tapestries in the palace are now equipped with special drop-cords, allowing them to be lowered off the walls quickly and safely. Members of the salvage team are now issued with two-way radios, allowing them to keep in constant touch with each other. There is also provision for them to give instructions to firemen about rescuing pieces of work from the heart of the fire zone.

The palace authorities are constantly engaged in assessing ways of improving the fire-detection and fire-control facilities. 'The fire at Windsor Castle following on so soon after the fire at Hampton Court has made everyone very conscious of these things,' explains Dennis McGuinnes. 'We have now installed the most up-to-date fire detection system available. We are still fine-tuning it, but the signs are good. The people who will be operating it – the warders – have confidence in it, and that is the important thing.'

Another recent innovation has been to introduce 'positive pressure fans'. These can clear smoke away from rooms adjacent to any fire, reducing smoke damage and allowing salvage teams to work unhindered by choking fumes. 'I was a bit sceptical to begin with,' admits Dennis. 'I couldn't understand how blowing air towards a fire could do any good at all. But I was very impressed by the tests. It really does work.'

CHAPTER 7

THE PEOPLE'S PALACE

*I*n 1838, the year Queen Victoria came to the throne, Lady Emily Montague died. She was the last of Hampton Court's Lady Housekeepers, and over the years she had taken a comfortable pension from the proceeds of allowing visitors to look over the palace. There were many who would have happily taken over her position. But the young Queen took a decisive step. She decided not to replace the late housekeeper. Instead she decreed that the palace should, henceforth, be open to the public without restriction and free of charge.

She appointed a new and very energetic Superintendent of Works, Edward Jesse, and a far-reaching programme of restoration and redecoration was at once begun. Under Mr Jesse's supervision the State Apartments were cleaned and refurbished. Tapestries and paintings were rehung – less to re-create the effect of the old interiors than to display a wide selection of the royal collection.

OPPOSITE Queen Victoria. ABOVE The window showing Henry VIII and his wives was a Victorian addition.

External repairs were also undertaken. The gatehouse, the West Front and the Great Hall were all returned to something approaching their Tudor glory; anachronistic sash windows, introduced during the previous century, were taken out and replaced with stone-mullioned latticed casements after the Tudor fashion. Georgian chimney stacks were taken down and replaced with red-brick substitutes.

The work of restoration and improvement continued throughout Victoria's long reign, gaining in sophistication and historical accuracy as it progressed. The Chapel windows were replaced, Anne Boleyn's Gateway was repaired, the moat along the West Front was re-dug, and the Wolsey Closet was created. The face of Henry VIII's astronomical clock was restored to its place. The Raphael cartoons, which had been returned to Hampton Court by George IV, were moved again: in 1865, to honour the memory of her late husband, Albert, the Queen ordered their removal to the

The palace chimneys and rooftops

South Kensington Museum (now the Victoria and Albert Museum). They were replaced, however, with tapestry versions of the same scenes.

The restoration work was appreciated by the public. In some quarters the Queen's decision to grant a more general access to the palace had been greeted with dire foreboding. It was supposed that the common herd might run riot through the building, pillaging on purpose what they did not destroy by accident. But such gloomy forecasts proved wholly inaccurate. The public proved respectful, interested and inquiring. The palace quickly developed into a popular place of excursion. The number of visitors, which had previously been counted in scant hundreds, rose at once to six figures. In 1839, the first year of free entry, 115,971 people visited the palace; by 1842 this

had risen to 179,743. An average of 220,000 was soon established and maintained.

Many came by road from London and its ever-spreading suburbs. Others came by river; it was a scenic route out along the Thames, and it allowed the visitors to avoid paying the toll to cross Kingston Bridge. The establishment, in 1849, of a branch of the South Western Railway, running from Waterloo to a station just across the river from the palace, had surprisingly little impact on numbers but did change the means by which the majority of visitors travelled.

The palace was closed on a Friday to allow the rooms to be cleaned, but it was open on every other day of the week. The most popular day for

Victorian visitors was Sunday. The palace was almost the only place of public resort within reach of London that was open on the Sabbath. In this the new provisions were merely following the existing practice; the Lady Housekeepers had never put a restriction on the visiting days, and Sundays had always been popular and, hence, remunerative. The policy, however, when made official, soon provoked the ire of the local Puritan element. The protests of the Sabbatarians were so vehement that – as one commentator noted – they 'could not have been more frantic had a visit to Hampton Court on Sunday been, not optional, but compulsory'. Personal letters were written to the Queen, invoking the memory of her 'pious grandfather'. The Rev. D. Wilson was moved to denounce the palace on a Sunday in the terms of Sodom and Gomorrah; it was, he claimed, 'a hell upon earth; the people come intoxicated, and the scenes in these gardens on the Lord's day are beyond description'. The force of his denunciation was slightly weakened when it was learnt that he had never visited Hampton Court.

In the face of such ill-informed attacks many hastened to defend the reputation of the Sunday visitors. The organist at the Chapel Royal asserted that he did not 'ever remember seeing a drunken character' on a Sunday. The wilder accusations of the Sabbatarians were countered: it was pointed out that since the palace did not open until two o'clock on a Sunday it did not constitute a rival to morning worship; and since the palace was closed on a Friday, the warders of the State Apartments were not denied their own day's rest each week. The storm was weathered, and Sunday opening was allowed to continue.

Hampton Court became a favoured resort for Victorian Londoners wanting a day away from the grime and noise of the capital.

The Maze, Hampton Court Palace

'Chestnut Sunday' became a London institution. On the middle Sunday in May thousands of trippers would come to admire the blossoming chestnut trees in the great avenue planted in Bushy Park by Sir Christopher Wren. Other areas of the garden had grown less happily. The elegant yew obelisks in the Great Fountain Garden had burgeoned into large dark umbrellas. The Wilderness, meanwhile, became something more closely approximating to its name, although the maze was preserved and became one of the great attractions of the place.

A vivid account of a late-Victorian excursion to Hampton Court is preserved in Jerome K. Jerome's classic work, *Three Men in a Boat*.

Harris recounts his visit to the maze with a country cousin. He had taken the precaution of studying a map of the maze, and had come to the prompt conclusion that, 'it was so simple that it seemed foolish – hardly worth the two pence charged for admission'. At the entrance to the maze he announced to his cousin his intention of just popping in for a quick 'walk round' before getting some lunch. Once inside they soon ran into some people, who said: 'they had been there for three quarters of an hour, and had had about enough of it. Harris told them they could follow him if they liked; he was just going in, and then should turn round and come out again. They said it was very kind of him, and fell behind, and followed.'

They picked up various other people who wanted to get it over, as they went along, until they absorbed all the persons in the maze. People who had given up all hopes of ever getting either in or out, or of ever seeing their home and friends again, plucked up courage at the sight of Harris and his party, and joined the procession, blessing him. Harris said he should judge there must have been

twenty people following him, in all; and one woman with a baby, who had been there all the morning, insisted on taking his arm, for fear of losing him.

Harris kept on with his policy of turning to the right at every junction, but they seemed no nearer to the centre. Doubts began to enter Harris's mind, and indeed the minds of his followers. There were murmurings of rebellion. At last, in exasperation, he produced his map. But it was pointed out that the map was of no use as they did not know where in the maze they were. A resolution was made to try to get back to the entrance. They set off with renewed hope and, after about ten minutes, found themselves in the centre.

Harris thought at first of pretending that that was what he had been aiming at; but the crowd looked dangerous, and he decided to treat it as an accident.

Anyhow, they had got something to start from then. They did know where they were, and the map was once more consulted, and the thing seemed simpler than ever, and off they started for the third time.

And three minutes later they were back in the centre again.

After that they simply couldn't get anywhere else. Whatever way they turned brought them back to the middle. It became so regular at length, that some of the people stopped there, and waited for the others to take a walk round, and come back to them. Harris drew out his map again, after a while, but the sight of it only infuriated the mob, and they told him to go and curl his hair with it. Harris said that he couldn't help feeling that, to a certain extent, he had become unpopular.

They all got crazy at last, and sang out for the keeper, and the man came and climbed up the ladder outside, and shouted out directions to them. But all their heads were, by this time, in such a confused whirl that they were incapable of grasping anything, and so the man told them to stop where they were, and he would come to them. They huddled together, and waited; and he climbed down, and came in.

He was a young keeper, as luck would have it, and new to the business; and when he got in, he couldn't get to them, and then *he* got lost. They caught sight of him, every now and then, rushing about the other side of the hedge, and he would see them, and rush to get to them, and they would wait there for about five minutes, and then he would reappear again in exactly the same spot, and ask them where they had been.

They had to wait until one of the old keepers came back from his dinner before they got out.

Harris said he thought it was a very fine maze, so far as he was a judge; and we agreed that we would try to get George to go into it, on our way back.

The arrival of Harris and the vulgar hordes rather disturbed the privacy of the grace-and-favour residents. Their own rooms – principally in the Base Court and the upper storeys above the State Apartments – were not, of course, open to the public, but the common areas of the palace were frequently thronged with people. To give the residents a place of retreat, the Privy Garden and Glass-Case Garden were allocated to their private

Once the Ladies' Playhouse, the King's Private Dining-Room was restored in 1992.

use. Both gardens retained a charm although they were much altered from their original conception. The Privy Garden had become a romantic jungle of towering shrubs and trees. The Tijou Screen had been removed from the far end of the garden, and a tennis court was made on the little triangle of ground between the garden and the river.

During the course of Queen Victoria's reign the prevailing character of the grace-and-favour residents became more elderly and female. This does not seem to have limited the variety and colourfulness of life within the community. Group activities flourished. There was an Amateur Dramatic Society – the King's Private Dining Room was converted into the 'Ladies' Playhouse'.

One of the late-Victorian residents was a Mrs Barclay. She attracted a good deal of adverse comment from her neighbours. At one point the palace Housekeeper felt obliged to write to the Lord Chamberlain stating, 'there have been complaints about Mrs Barclay. I should tell you confidentially that Mrs Barclay drinks and keeps her pigwash in a cupboard on the public staircase. Mrs Barclay's language and behaviour is such that no respectable person will remain in her service. I live in dread of my servants being contaminated.'

A rather less troublesome resident was Princess Frederica of Hanover, a young cousin of the Queen, who, together with her husband Baron von Pawel Rammingen, was granted a suite of rooms in 1880. While at the palace the Princess gave birth to a daughter, but the baby died almost immediately. In the wake of this tragedy she decided to establish a convalescent home for young mothers. To raise funds for the project she got the Queen's permission to host a charity gala in the Great Hall. Two plays were performed and more than 500 people attended.

FORWARD INTO THE PAST

Since Victoria's time the great palace has enjoyed a slow evolution along the lines established during her reign. Much has remained the same and much has altered only slightly. Admission – alas – is no longer free. The policy of granting grace-and-favour residencies at Hampton Court was discontinued at the beginning of the 1970s, but a few residents still live on in some of the apartments. Other suites are now being used as accommodation for people working at the palace. Hampton Court has also become a very suitable home to several important organizations: the Embroiderers' Guild, the Royal School of Needlework and the Textile Conservation Centre.

Nor has Hampton Court lost altogether its close association with royalty. In November 1982 Queen Beatrix of the Netherlands, while on a state visit to Britain, hosted a banquet at the palace for Queen Elizabeth II. And the same year Princess Anne was the guest of honour at a dinner given in the Great Hall by the Royal College of Surgeons. Henry VIII's magnificent Hall also provided the setting for Prince Charles's famous 'carbuncle' speech on the horrors of modern architecture.

The process of refurbishment and restoration, of returning the rooms, courts and gardens to their original – or most characteristic – form has continued. Many treasures have been returned to the palace. The great fire of 1986, despite its toll of devastation, did allow for the substantial restoration of the King's Apartments. And this has now been matched by the brilliantly researched re-creation of William III's Privy Garden, in place of the overgrown shrubbery which had sprung up to obscure the great south façade of Wren's block.

The palace is better maintained and visitors are better served than ever before. There are some 370 members of staff at the palace. Restaurants and cafeterias have been opened. Imaginative displays and recorded tours are available to help bring the palace to life. The guides are better informed – and better mannered – than their historical predecessors. (One early-seventeenth-century visitor to the palace complained of the custodian of the 'Paradise' room, 'It is strange that the keeper of this room is so sordid that you must bargain beforehand about his fee; yet from his dress he appears a grand gentleman.') From the period dress of some of the present guides you might conclude that they were anything from a Tudor lady-in-waiting to a late-seventeenth-century gentleman.

The number of visitors continues to grow; in 1997 over 680,000 people paid to see the palace. Perhaps as many as two million visited the gardens.

Although the end of grace-and-favour accommodation has reduced the number of people living in the palace, Hampton Court still serves as a home form many staff members. There are plans too to increase the number of residents. 'We have been looking at the possibility of letting some of the apartments commercially,' admits Dennis McGuinnes, the Deputy Director. It would be a very desirable address. 'We want to keep Hampton Court as a living palace,' says Dennis. 'The one word we won't hear about the palace is "museum". It is much, much more than that.'

A view across the restored Privy Garden; the statue of Bacchus is a copy.

INDEX

ACKNOWLEDGEMENTS

Bazal would like to thank Nick Aarons, Emma Beckwith, Nikki Cheetham, Annette Clark, Tim Cragg, Susan Crook, Jenn Feray, Justine Field, Claire Hobday, Claire Howell, Paul Jenkins, Joe Orr, Ben Philpott, Louise Rainbow, John Reddin, Charlotte Reid, Jamie Reid, Mark Robinson and Graeme Towner for their work on the television series.

Channel 4 Books would like to thank Robin Evans, Edward Impey and Clare Murphy at Hampton Court Palace and Edward Hewlett, Shruti Patel and Nicole Tetzner at the Royal Collection.

Especial thanks to everyone working at Hampton Court Palace who has contributed to the series and the book especially Robert Allen, Caroline Allington, Vivienne Andrews, Jenny Band, James Boulding, Tony Boulding, Dennis Burge, Simon Burge, Lucy Capito, Kevin Coates, Craig Cowell, Joe Cowell, Gillian Cox, Graham Dillamore, Elizabeth Elvin, Richard Evans, Anne Fletcher, Lucy Fotheringham, Ian Franklin, Donna Gelardi, Terry Gough, Claire Hanham, Anna Harrison, Allan Hubbard, Gerald Humphreys, Dennis McGuinnes, Adrian Phillips, Chris Ronaldson, Lesley Ronaldson, Ivan Ronaldson, Ted Salisbury, Lynsay Shephard, Helen Smith, Tina Soliss, Leslie Strudwick and Gary Wise.

On the historical side the author would like to acknowledge a debt to Ernest Law's magisterial three-volume *The History of Hampton Court Palace* (1888) which has informed all studies of the palace for the last hundred years. Of more recent works, Simon Thurley's *Royal Palaces of Tudor England* (Yale University Press, 1993) was particularly useful.

The Royal Collection, a vast array of works of art of all kinds, is owned by The Queen as Sovereign in trust for Her successors and the nation. Items from the Royal Collection can be seen at the thirteen palaces, castles and houses open to the public. In addition, a large number of items are loaned every year to exhibitions worldwide.

PICTURE CREDITS

Crown copyright: Historic Royal Palaces. Reproduced by permission of Historic Royal Palaces under licence from the Controller of Her Majesty's Stationery Office: 1, 5, 6, 7, 12, 14, 15, 17, 27, 34, 42(L), 42(R), 48–9, 69, 70, 76, 81, 91, 116, 122, 126–7, 133(L), 133(R), 135, 137, 151, 152, 159, 165, 168–9, 180, 183, 184, 185, 187. Jan Baldwin: 33, 44, 150, 155, 156. Earl Beesley: 26, 32, 37, 43, 117, 126, 128, 129, 132, 173. Martin Beddall: 170. Cliff Birtchnell: 16(L), 16(R), 28, 29, 47, 175.

Jerry Young © GMG Endemol Entertainment: 2–3, 10–11, 20, 22, 23, 24, 31, 35, 60, 62–3, 64, 66, 86, 88, 89, 103, 106, 108, 109, 111, 112, 114, 115, 120, 131, 134, 138, 140, 141, 142, 143, 144, 145, 146, 148, 149, 162–3, 166, 174, 176, 178, 179, 181, 189.

The Royal Collection © Her Majesty The Queen: 9 (406107), 30, 90 (402842), 121 (403983), 182 (405131). Stephen Chapman: 19 (404746), 41 (404742), 68 (404441), 71 (404739), 75 (405749), 95 (402853), 118(L) (405675), 118(R) (405674), 136 (405614), 153 (404390), 157 (404413). A.C. Cooper Ltd: 52–3 (405796), 78 (405887), 93 (405353), 96–7 (405791), 123 (404760). Antonia Reeve: 24–5 (1079), 77 (401224). Geoffrey Shakerley: 100 (403960). Rodney Todd-White: 94 (407247).

© IMG Arts and Entertainment: 56, 58, 59.

Holder Swan Public Relations: 84.

Paul Dyer/Marney Hall: 82. Carl Wallace: 85.